T0160292

Selling is So Easy, It's Hard

Selling is So Easy, It's Hard

77 Ways Salespeople Shoot Themselves in the Wallet

Dr. Gary S. Goodman

Published 2019 by Gildan Media LLC
aka G&D Media
www.GandDmedia.com

Front Cover design by David Rheinhardt of Pyrographx

Interior design by Meghan Day Healey of Story Horse, LLC

Library of Congress Cataloging-in-Publication Data is available upon request

ISBN: 978-1-7225-0194-5

10   9   8   7   6   5   4   3   2   1

Contents

Introduction

I was watching one of my clients deliver a pep talk to his salespeople. A former Marine, the speaker was a blunt instrument.

"Discipline is the most important thing in life!" he bellowed to youngsters half his age.

I didn't think he was getting his point across, but I was hoping to hear something I could use.

I had the feeling he hired me as a sales consultant partly because he wanted someone to compete against. A worthy adversary, a foil, someone he could disprove, a PhD and noted author to whom he could show a thing or two.

But that didn't matter. I had surprised more than one cocky client during my consulting career.

They say a broken clock is accurate at least twice a day, and this rough-and-tumble fellow was about to prove the point. With one sentence, he made me come to attention.

"Selling is so easy, it's hard," he said.

Selling *is* easy, I thought. Talk to enough people, and ask them all to buy. Some will do it. What could be easier than that?

Yet selling is hard. Why do so few people rise to the top and stay on top in this profession? How come there are so many flashes in the pan, people who get off to a great start and then fizzle into obscurity and evaporate into outright failure? What is it that prevents people from doing this simple deed—selling successfully—day after day, year after year?

It's an easy occupation, but judging from the rampant turnover in the ranks of salespeople, it is hard. It frowns upon far more folks than it smiles upon.

It reminds me a lot of baseball. Seasoned veterans are fond of saying, "Sooner or later, baseball will make a fool of everyone." You have it figured out, and then it tricks you. You're slumping. Can't buy a hit or even scrape by on a walk or an error. Every pitcher seems to have your number.

In the sales field, prospects spot you a mile away. You suffer from "sales breath." Every syllable, word and intonation reeks of insincerity and self-centeredness. I've been a salesperson, a sales manager, a business owner, and a sales consultant. I've written some of the best-selling books in the sales field. I've made thousands of sales and millions of dollars doing it.

And yet until now, I've never really figured out why some sellers succeed, are built to last, while others, even more talented and gifted, fail.

I'll tell you the great secret: salespeople defeat themselves.

I've seen it happen. It has happened to my recruits and trainees. And it has happened to me.

My first observation of self-defeating sales behavior occurred in my own home, when I was growing up. My father was a professional salesman. Though he had various prestigious occupational titles that might lead you to think otherwise, his main focus was always selling. But he wasn't your typical huckster or carnival barker. He was very low-key, a polished communicator. He had earned a BA in liberal arts from a solid university, and he almost completed a law degree. He could have been and done a number of things. But selling was his calling. He was hooked on it.

He fell into a self-destructive pattern that was noticeable to nearly everyone but him. It lasted for his entire professional life. It would usher in periods of feast and famine. Obviously this was hard on him, but it also took a toll on his family. He'd rise to the top in a given company, and then suddenly he'd quit, ostensibly over a misunderstanding he'd have with his boss.

He wanted to be acknowledged, to be appreciated for all of the heavy lifting he was doing. Yet he also wanted to be left alone, to set his own hours, and to get the job done his way. He wanted too much, especially on an emotional level—more than a sales job could give him.

When things were good and he was selling well, we lived beautifully. We had impressive houses in the best neighborhoods. Between jobs, which seemed to occur way too frequently, we would be shuttled to tiny apartments without the best amenities.

This is not to say my dad was without talent. He was a gifted salesperson. I can say this with authority, because I would hear him prospect over the phone from the house. He had an uncanny ability to adjust from one prospect to the next. His prospects adored him, and whatever he was doing, it paid the bills. He got good results when he wasn't sabotaging his success.

I won't go into detail here about his specific techniques. I have noted some of them in my book, *How to Sell Like a Natural Born Salesperson*. But when you add up his miscues, along with mine and those of thousands of other sellers I've worked with and trained over the years, they can be distilled into 77 tips.

If you don't use these pointers, you'll shoot yourself in the wallet, sacrificing millions of dollars of earnings during your career, and you'll doom yourself and those that care about you to a lifestyle far less satisfying and far more painful than you and they deserve.

Fortunately, some of these worst practices won't be vexing you. Skip around the following pages, if you like. I'm sure you'll discover that you're mired in some invisible habits that will take your breath away once you realize they are your Achilles' heels.

The good news is we can all change, we can improve, and we can realize more of our full potential. Here's to a more satisfying and rewarding career and lasting success!

77 Tips to Keep from Shooting Yourself in the Wallet

Tip 1: Find the Right Sales Opportunities for You!

Many salespeople fail to reach their potential because they've taken on an inappropriate sales job. It's a bad fit for them.

You won't find this point in any of the sales books I've read or written. Nobody talks about it, but it is exceedingly important.

My first sales job was at age ten. I delivered newspapers. Of course, it wasn't a good sales job. It was pretty much all you could get if you were ten. Still, it was a bad fit because I didn't see it as selling. I believed it was about delivery, about balancing papers on my handlebars and getting them delivered without plunking them into puddles.

The real money was in tips. If you could figure out a way to get a nice tip, especially around Christmas, you could be in clover.

Some of my friends did it. They would sweet-talk their customers whenever they saw them. In some cases, they asked where the best place was to put the paper, on the porch or in the mailbox. "Would you like me to ring your bell to let you know it's here?" they would inquire sweetly. All of these touches led to big tips.

I would not do any of it.

You could say customer service wasn't my strong suit. It is ironic that this would become one of my career interests. (Read all about it at my website: www.customer satisfaction.com.)

Back to newspaper delivery: if my customers didn't complain, and I got home before dark, I was just fine.

A much better fit was selling papers on busy street corners, when the products were literally hot off the presses. That's when you made tips from the big spenders looking for how their stocks performed at the close of the market. I could also choose my clients by walking up to them or by striding into their office buildings.

There were definite ways I could leverage my time and my effectiveness—a key to winning in any sales work.

Tip 2: Choose the Best Sales Medium for You

My first real sales job was at Time-Life Books, when I was nineteen. It played to several of my strengths and interests. I was working my way through college, so the hours were great. In fact, I heard about the job at the school's employment board.

It was also a phone job. I've always had a mature voice, but for my first few decades I also had a baby face. The latter didn't help me to interact with older buyers, but my voice enabled me to relate well to everyone.

Choosing your selling medium is critical. Later, I would sell in person and on the phone. I'd take airplanes to visit clients when necessary. But my first love was and still is the phone.

Where are you at your best: in front of people or at a distance?

I ran a telephone sales seminar in Chicago in which a fellow strode to the podium to share a secret with me. He said he was a great seller outdoors, at people's offices. But whenever his sales manager planned a phone blast, where field salespeople were brought together in a bullpen to contact prospects, he broke into a cold sweat.

He suffered from phone fear. It's like stage fright, if you have to act, or speech anxiety, if you're delivering a talk to a group. It is a special form of situational shyness, and in extreme cases, it can feel so threatening that you become deskilled. Your mouth fills with cotton, and you fail to summon the right words.

If you know this about yourself, it makes sense to avoid a sales job that requires heavy phone work.

But isn't that admitting a weakness? Yes it is, but this is a lot better than gritting your teeth and suffering.

Play to your strengths. If you're great in front of people, maybe you should hire a sales assistant to place your calls and to set your appointments. This will be a person who loves phoning, right?

Tip 3: Be Sure Your Pay Plan Makes Sense to You and Feels Right

I know a salesman who tried to sell precious metals—gold, silver, and platinum—from a breathtakingly beautiful office facing the superblue Pacific Ocean. This place was so gorgeous that he didn't want to leave, even to have lunch. There was a terrace with director's chairs and a table so employees could bask in the California sun.

The problem was there was no money to be made. The market for metals was dead. Worse, the stock market was soaring, giving prospects for metals real returns that made headlines every day.

On a straight commission pay plan, my friend had to eat, and this meant making sales. But the only leads available were old and weak, not worth pursuing. No one bought.

He couldn't believe that he made zero sales, and it took him ten weeks without pay to admit that he had chosen the wrong sales job. Making matters worse, the straight commission pay plan drove him nuts. He was one of those people that need a guaranteed salary. It can be a salary plus commissions, or a draw against commissions, but there needs to be definite money that will go toward paying the bills.

Are you this way? How much security do you need? How much income risk are you willing to bear?

I mentioned someone that failed under a straight

commission compensation plan. But there must be others that succeed, correct?

One of my financial-industry clients in Houston sold government bond funds to major banks, universities, and other institutional investors. All of its salespeople were on a straight commission pay plan.

Within a month or two, the great majority of them brought in their first orders. They had been cold-calling and sending out brochures and prospectuses, so their pipelines were filling with prospects.

Accepted wisdom holds that if you fill your pipeline and keep making calls and presentations, you will earn your share of sales. Then you might experience a gusher, like an oil well that bursts into being and keeps pumping commissions into your pockets.

But one fellow had been diligently feeding the pipe for ten months, and not even a drop trickled out the other end. He earned no sales—*nada*. Where others had sales numbers to post at the front of the room, he was the not-so-proud owner of a big goose egg.

How would you feel if you labored for ten months and hadn't earned a penny? You would have left the scene long before that, right? That would have been logical and rational, don't you agree?

He stayed.

One day, when I was there, doing some training of new recruits, the spell was broken.

He earned his first sale. It was a major Japanese bank that awarded this gentleman with his first deal and his first commission.

How much did he make?

He made $1 million. Let me repeat that. *He made 1 million bucks on his first sale!*

This story is of course about patience and perseverance. It is about believing in yourself and in your product. It is about 1001 things. But the main insight I want you to have is to ask, how much are you like this fellow? Could you hold out for ten months until earning your first dollar in that company? Would your family and friends let you do it? Do you have the funds to stay afloat in case your ship is very late in arriving?

I've had my own consulting and training business for decades. I am paid on a straight commission basis as well. It is a feast or famine situation. I can handle it if I am a prudent planner and otherwise financially responsible.

Are you? Most people are not. They live from paycheck to paycheck. They would like to see fatter paychecks, but they *must* see steady ones. That's how they're wired psychologically. They would settle for a much lower income, providing it is steady and it feels safe.

The great behavioral psychologist B.F. Skinner said that when it comes to rewards, "the *schedule* of the reward is more important than the amount" in determining our performances.

You may like the "juice," as some call it—the thrill of *not* knowing what your pay will be during a given interval. This is the same juice that gamblers find so appealing, and it is the juice that creates addictions.

Be honest with yourself. How are you wired? If you were on a straight commission pay plan would this be

OK, would it excite you, or would it eat at you, riddling you with uncertainty and anxiety?

Sales compensation is often negotiable. You can negotiate how much you are paid. You can also negotiate *when* you're paid—daily, weekly, or monthly. You can also negotiate the proportion of fixed versus variable pay, the parts that are guaranteed and the parts that are based on sales outcomes.

Some of the wisest companies give sellers a choice. You can get a set salary, nicely and predictably, although your commissions will not be as generous as they would be if you elected a straight commission formula. But it is your call.

Every so often, you can even have a chance to jump from one plan to the next. Say you are just starting, and you don't know how much you'll earn. You could select the salary plus commission. After several pay cycles, you might make the leap to a straight commission, because you will have experienced success the other way.

Whatever you do, *don't work under a pay plan that is demotivating.*

Tip 4: Script Your Success

I mentioned that selling is easy, and it can be, if you have a proven plan for getting prospects to say yes. If you don't have a repeatable routine, then you're definitely going to shoot yourself in the wallet.

You need to script your success, because scripts work. If you're using one and it doesn't get more sales than improvisation accomplishes, then it is a poor script and you should improve it.

Make changes until it is a money machine.

One of the best reasons to follow a script is that it is usually the shortest path to a sale. There are countless ways to NOT earn an order, but a script delivers one that consistently achieves positive outcomes. It eliminates a lot of fluff from your conversation, reducing the chance that you'll inadvertently blurt out something stupid that will kill a sale.

Known as the *KISS method*, a script requires you to *Keep It Simple, Salesperson*.

I consulted for a company that brought aboard a half-dozen salespeople who were all allowed to say what they wanted and to make up their sales talks on the fly. In every case, they failed. Each one overtalked, making what should have been a brief and pleasant walk in the park into a painful slog through the brambles.

I came in and streamlined the process. I tested my call paths and made sales quickly. In fact, my first deal landed the most profitable client in the firm's history.

Why guess when you can know?

The shortest route is a direct line between two points, correct? Why would anyone want to take detours, most of which lead to dead ends?

If they're self-defeating salespeople, that's the best way to get their secret wish, which is failure and frustration.

Salespeople fight scripts by coming up with a lot of bogus objections to using them. They say:

Scripts sound phony!

A script will make me sound robotic.

If you feel this way, I have news for you. You are probably using a script now without realizing it.

Certain words and phrases are being repeated from presentation to presentation. But they haven't been tested and proven objectively to work for you instead of against you.

For example, by overtalking, one of the reps at the company I just mentioned would repeatedly produce interruptions and objections. Then he would ask: "What are your specific concerns about developing a relationship with us?"

He evoked a general objection to continuing the conversation, and then he asked people to offer even more specific reasons for resisting the offer and him. He would repeat this self-defeating process call after call. It *was* a script, but it was a prescription for failure.

If you don't have a winning script, observe someone who is selling what you're selling and doing a great job of it, earning tons of dough. Write down what you're hearing, and then refine it. If you don't have a great role model on the scene, hire a coach or consultant.

Tip 5: Avoid Secondary-Gain Traps

Our job as salespeople is to earn as much money as we can, for ourselves and for our companies. This is our primary gain, our chief objective. Anything that we do on the job that feels rewarding but doesn't contribute directly to making said profits is a secondary gain.

For instance, we may enjoy speaking to prospects. Inevitably we'll hit it off with one or two who always have a smile or a joke or a warm welcome for us. We'll gravitate toward them, finding excuses to contact them, even if we have nothing to sell them. Deep down, we know they are never, ever going to purchase from us. We are hoping to get sales, but we're doing things that distract us from accomplishing that end.

Once when I was running a seminar in Texas, a fellow said: "I refuse to sell someone unless he has become my friend first!"

I asked him to clarify. He went on to say that friendship came first and sales second. That is a perfect example of someone that was mired in a secondary-gain trap.

Above, I urged you to script your sales presentations. Let's say you suspected that scripts worked well to produce sales, but you didn't like using one because it would become boring to you to keep saying the same old things. In that case, you'd be putting entertainment and diversion and even the secret thrill of failure ahead of the primary gain of earning profits and paychecks.

Secondary-gain traps are everywhere! Watch out for them!

Tip 6: Always Ask for the Sale!

Asking for the sale is known in the trade as *closing*. Those that have no qualms about asking for the order are often called *closers*.

Closers earn a lot more than nonclosers.

Those that don't ask for the sale are losers.

Why will a salesperson speak to a prospect and then fail to ask for the order?

We know sellers do lots of irrational things—77 of them, to be precise. This is one of the very worst habits—failing to ask for the deal.

Some sellers don't ask because they're afraid to hear no. They've been brought up to be nonconfrontational, and when someone refuses their offer, these sellers feel they are being rejected personally. That hurts the ego, and people protect their fragile egos with defense mechanisms. Not asking for a yes means that you're also not asking for a no. This results in elongated relationships with nonbuyers. It is a huge waste of time.

Closing—asking for a yes—is the fastest way to qualify and disqualify a prospect, to determine if he or she is seriously interested in doing business. If someone won't say yes to a conditional close, they aren't worth pursuing.

Example: A car salesperson walks up to a person who has been gazing at the inventory. "Do you see anything you like?" the seller inquires.

"Not so far."

"What are you looking for?"

"A, B, and C."

"If I can find you a car with A, B, and C, can you drive it home today?"

"I suppose."

"Well, let's track one down for you, OK?"

Some methods of closing are better than others. But in every case, the seller should believe several things to make closing efforts effective.

For one thing, sellers must believe they have a valuable and desirable product. Second, they need to believe owning that product will benefit the buyer. And third, the seller must be willing to make the buying decision on behalf of the prospect, if and when necessary.

The third part, deciding FOR the buyer, is crucial in closing, because most people will not close themselves. They won't quickly and efficiently purchase without being directly influenced by the seller.

"Nice car, right?"

"Yes, it is."

"OK, let's do the paperwork. My desk is right over here. Can I get you a coffee or a soft drink?"

I was listening to a sales manager as he trained new hires. He said, "I don't care how much you think you've blown a deal, or how little you have earned it. Promise me, and promise yourself you'll do one thing before the conversation ends. Ask for the sale at least once!"

Closing should be a habit and a reflex. In fact, you should have some set phrases that will work in most situations:

So let's move forward, and I know you'll be pleased, OK?

This looks great in green, or would you prefer the blue?

I'll email the paperwork within the next hour. Get that signed and faxed back to me this afternoon, and your loan will fund tomorrow, OK?

These closes are engineered to produce a buying reflex. Many of them have an "OK?" at the end. When you ask, "OK?" people are inclined to reflexively respond in kind. Sometimes referred to as *tie-downs*, they secure the order.

Closes are also necessary when answering an objection. Imagine a customer says that something costs too much. Start with an agreement, a phrase that says, "Well, I appreciate that, but . . ." or "Well, I know what you mean, but . . ."

You can also use the "feel-felt-found" reply: "I understand how you *feel*, and a number of people have *felt* that, but they've *found* . . ."

The next step in handling the objection is to address the content, to rebut the claim the objection is making: "But they've found that this gizmo actually pays for itself within two years, and after that, it's free."

The final step in addressing the objection is to close off of the answer you supplied.

"So let's move forward, and I know you'll be pleased, OK?"

Again, we append a close to relieve the buyer of making the decision on his or her own. We decide for them. We get the ball rolling.

Here is how the three parts come together:

"It seems expensive to me," the customer says.

"Well, I understand how you feel, and a number of folks have felt that, but they've found that this pays for itself in two years, and then it's free, so let's move forward, and I know you'll be pleased, OK?"

I have a catchphrase to offer you:

When in doubt, close it out.

Let's say you've been going back and forth having a lively conversation with the prospect. Suddenly there is a silence.

That's your cue to close.

Or you've told the person enough to make a good buying decision. Close at that point.

"Well, I guess that's all you really need to know, so let's wrap this up, and I'm sure you'll be pleased, OK?"

Choosing the best words requires skill and knowledge. Applying them, actually closing, calls for discipline.

Close habitually, or your earnings will suffer.

Tip 7: Before Cutting Your Prices, Defend Them

Every company must earn a profit, or it cannot survive, or afford to pay you. Every time a prospect gets you to cut your prices, he or she imperils your job and your pocketbook.

So price cutting is dangerous. It's also a bad practice to sell a low price, because someone, somewhere, will undercut your prices and steal sales away.

What's the alternative?

Sell value.

Let me offer a radical example. You may have heard of the Bugatti Veyron, one of the most powerful cars in the world. It has something like 1001 horsepower. By comparison, I own a Porsche V-8 that only has 340 horses. The Veyron costs between $1.8 million and $2.8 million. A set of replacement tires will run you about $25,000, a bargain compared to changing the oil, which is about $21,000. Amazing, right? How can a seller justify such astronomical prices?

You have to sell value. This includes exclusivity. Very few people outside of billionaires can afford to own a Veyron. You enter a very elite club when you purchase this item. Plus, these cars are exciting to drive. You'll be noticed. People will treat you better, with more respect.

I could go on, as you can imagine. Who wants to be just another boring Ferrari owner when you can leave these mere pedestrians in the dust?

The same logic applies to selling practically any item. Justify your margins. They're necessary.

A profit isn't a bauble, an ornament, a frill. It is a condition of being in business tomorrow.

One retort to this idea is that certain items are commodities, meaning you can buy them anywhere. So the only competitive advantage left to sellers in achieved by discounting one's price. That's the only way someone will select and prefer you.

I don't buy it, because nothing is ONLY a commodity.

Take one of the businesses a client of mine is in: copper wire. Copper is copper, and wire is wire, correct? Nothing sexy about it, is there? But there can be remarkable differences in the customer service offered by company A versus company B. One may be extremely pleasant to interact with, and the other may go out of its way to offend. Let's say the polite company charges

5 percent more than the grouch. Is it worth a 5 percent premium to have a good and pleasant relationship?

For certain buyers, it is absolutely worth extra.

While it is generally true that in a capitalistic society, competition will lower prices over time, it is part of your sales job to keep inventing and delivering buyer satisfactions that you can point to that will justify your prices.

If you want to shorten your career, and empty your savings account, do the opposite. Cut prices by cutting your commissions. Next, management will cut you.

Tip 8: Follow Through or You'll Be Blue!

I don't know of any salesman who wouldn't rejoice if every prospect said a definitive yes or no to offers immediately. How efficient that would be, and how clarifying! What a timesaver!

It is a fact of life that different buyers have different buying schedules. Some make snap decisions. Others take time to comparison-shop and to let their buying fervor dissipate.

Others are simply laggards, slowpokes who take forever to arrive at a yes or no.

To maximize our effectiveness, we have to figure out a way to adjust to these different timetables. Customer-relationship management (CRM) systems are crucial because they compel us to follow through with nearly everyone. One of my clients has a rule that is embedded into its client-tracking software: you must follow up eight times before classifying a contact as permanently unreachable or unsellable.

Of course, if among those contacts someone has flat-out said no, he's not interested, then you can note this and be relieved of having to make further contact. But that lead will be reassigned in thirty days, after the prospect has cooled off, and that newly assigned rep will then be required to make eight selling attempts.

This routine, which can be tedious and even time-wasting, actually produces some interesting outcomes. For one thing, it forces salespeople to squeeze the value from all prospects that enter the system. Leads, which are often costly, receive due and sufficient attention. The system also forces sellers to do enough work to justify earning business even from the slowest of laggards, not just from the quick closes.

Reassigning deals after one rep has failed to close a prospect brings a new personality into the equation. This T-O, or turning over to a new face or voice, can work wonders. The next pairing of buyer and seller may really like each other.

However, being exhaustive with your prospects requires ample time and energy. And there is always the question of effectiveness. Would you be better served to cut bait earlier and to focus your attention ONLY on new prospects?

It's hard to say. If you have ample and inexhaustible stores of leads, then you may be able to cherry-pick. But this situation is rare. It's more common to have scarce leads, so few that you have to milk each one for all it can yield. This occurs in maturing industries.

Whenever a new service is being marketed, typically there is a wide-open audience for it. Lots of leads, and cheap ones at that, are available. But seeing and hearing about the riches to be had, competitors flood the field. Lead costs soar, which disables sellers with poor closing skills. At the same time, price competition enters the scene, squeezing profits even more.

So don't count on a "There's more where they came from" mentality to see you through. Expect scarce leads, and be prepared to follow through more than you'd like.

An incidental benefit of incessant follow-though is it will make you appreciate it all the more when new leads are assigned to you. You'll swarm them.

Tip 9: Be Willing to Cut Bait

You may think I'm contradicting myself. I just said you need to follow through more than you will want to do. Now we switch gears.

Let's say you have been following through trying to edge your prospects into the closed zone. But they're stuck where they are, and you're feeling no progress.

You might want to ease off for a few days or weeks, and then mix it up with them some more. Or you might push for clarity, wondering if there's any hope for them.

One strategy I use is to ask them if they're worth pursuing.

"From your vantage point, do you think we're headed in the right direction? Are we going to do some business together?"

Or you can use what I call a reverse-empathic question:

"If you were in my shoes, would you invest any more effort in following up with you?"

One client of mine, who purchased a profitable training program from me, commented as I was leaving her site for the last time: "Thanks for your persistence!"

She was grateful that I had hung in there with her until she green-lit our project. But I assigned too much significance to her comment. I told myself, "See, you need to keep pushing even those prospects that seem like they'll never buy!" This is simply not true.

With some and perhaps with many prospects, a point comes when you need to cut bait, let them go.

Would some of them buy if you kept chasing them? The answer is yes, but their value would be less than the value we throw away in relentlessly pursuing them.

By the way, that client who expressed gratitude was impossible to resell. I persisted again after I delivered the original program, but I never evoked her second thank you.

Tip 10: Don't Worry about Results

It is important to set goals. They give us something to aim at. They're motivating. They hold us accountable, and they provide a neat, numerical way to track our results and our effectiveness. But they shouldn't induce destructive anxiety, as in "There's no way I'm going to hit my targets!" or "I'm way off my sales plan—if this keeps up I'll really be in trouble!"

Stressing about results can easily distract you from carrying out the processes that lead to results. In a word, when we're worrying, we can't be working at the same time. One activity displaces the other. On the upside, this means that when you're busy working, it's very hard to worry.

I see the negative impact of worrying on new hires. Their number-one question is "Am I going to succeed here?" They make inferences about their probable success with scant information. They may be in training before they've been activated, yet they're stressing about what they're being asked to do, because they perceive that the techniques won't work.

One fellow I know couldn't get over the fact that the average telephone presentation lasted for forty-five to seventy-five minutes, and it was highly scripted. He thought he'd never get through it. This feeling gnawed at him even though there were several successful role models on the sales floor that were doing it word for word, day in and day out. He did graduate from training, but he split after a day or two of restless dialing. His obsession over results destroyed his chances of succeeding at that place of business.

Keep your sights on work processes. Don't make things more complicated or more daunting than they are.

If the job has been well designed and the market for and pricing of your products has been well defined, you should succeed. Let the results come as they may.

Tip 11: Don't Be a Mind Reader

One of my professors, the mighty management sage Peter F. Drucker, had an interesting take on selling. He said, "If you do a good enough job of marketing, selling becomes unnecessary."

Before you retort, "Selling is ALWAYS necessary!" consider what he meant.

He meant if you have very carefully come to know who your ideal buyers are and their budgets and preferences, and you get your message across to them, you shouldn't have to twist their arms to make them purchase. This sounds a little like "Build a better mousetrap, and people will beat a path to your door," but there is some truth in it.

Unfortunately, most employers that you'll sell for are not very good at marketing. So at best you'll waste a certain amount of your resources. This is inevitable. In other cases, you'll need to tailor your presentations to create a better fit.

But you should never prejudge who is going to buy and who will not.

For years, I had this prejudice against insurance companies. Somewhere, somehow I had determined that they simply weren't worth selling, that they were too stodgy, too cheap, and too costly to woo. So I would avoid marketing to them when I promoted my sales and customer-service seminars around the country.

Lo and behold, guess what happened.

A few years ago, I received an inquiry from a reader of my book *Monitoring, Measuring, and Managing Cus-*

tomer Service. She was the chief operating officer of a regional insurance agency, and she went on to purchase a half-million dollars' worth of services from me. As I was completing that contract, I sold another insurance company a $750,000 deal.

Whoa! Those contracts made me reconsider.

What's funny is that that very bias against insurance companies recurred when I was testing a sales program for a client. I came across some insurance-agency leads and I thought, "They'll never buy!" Yet among my first ten sales was one to an insurance agency.

We never know who will ultimately say yes. I just got a contract emailed to me for a sizable amount from a health-care company that I had almost completely written off.

Nowadays, I ignore the part of my CRM software that asks me to predict the likelihood that I'll close a given prospect. Frankly, you never know, and it is truly wasteful to guess. Put the energy you'd waste to work following through with everyone. That will give you a better return on your time.

Tip 12: Don't Bring Your Friends

If you have been in sales for a while, you've held plenty of mediocre and outright lousy jobs. You've also commiserated with a number of congenial salespeople who have been in the same boat, working where you worked.

Perhaps you made a pact to stay in touch, and if a good thing comes along, to notify each other.

Suddenly, you're in clover, working a new job that's not only paying the bills but leaving something extra in your pocket. You're thrilled, and you can't wait to share your good fortune with the underprivileged folks you left behind at those inferior places. After all, some of these colleagues, like you, were really good at sales, and they deserve to spend some time basking in the warm glow of success, as you are doing. Plus, you'll feel wonderful if you let them in on your good news.

There's even a bonus. Your new employer offers a referral spiff for people you bring in. So what's to stop you from doing a pal or two some good while pocketing an extra buck?

I'm going to stop you, because bringing them in may be harmful to your wallet and to your career.

What a killjoy! Here you get a chance to howl about your good fortune, and I want to muzzle you. What gives?

First, leads are finite, no matter what you think. Your current company is set up to give you 100 fresh leads per month. Let's say you were the first hire, and your buddy, the one you are bringing in, will be the second. What is to stop your company from splitting your 100 leads fifty-fifty?

Oh, I know that may not happen on day one. But once it appears your friend has talent, management will have to feed him too. Where will his leads come from?

That's easy, you think. They'll just order more leads, so there will be enough for all.

It doesn't work like that. Companies are greedy, and they want to see you two get hungry and feed on each other. That will motivate both of you. You'll outdo your personal best. Your pal will imitate you, and earn opportunities that were once entirely yours.

Were you the firstborn in your household, and then two, three, or four siblings came along? At first you had 100 percent of the attention and the goodies, and then you had the privilege of raising the newbies and keeping them in line, correct?

The same thing occurs in companies. You'll be taking a pay cut if leads are suddenly rationed, and any little spiff the company gave you will seem miniscule given the sales that you'll forgo. Plus, you'll be mentoring your new arrivals.

My reasoning isn't restricted to you being first at the scene. You could be the twenty-fifth seller who is being asked to refer your capable pals.

Don't do it.

Politics can also hurt you. You and that guy or gal you ushered in are now seen as a mated pair. If there is a layoff, or a cutback, management will be likely to show both of you the door.

What if your friends FAIL? What if they don't make it? Will you be perceived differently?

Bet on it. The new you will be damaged goods if you recruit a loser. If this happens, you can also dash your hopes for moving up into sales management.

Plus, why bring in a security risk? Loose lips sink ships, and your buddy may be a gossip, telling tales about your past. Do you really need your reputation called into question?

If successful, your colleague will put others to shame, imperiling the jobs of those that were on the scene before he or she arrived. That will put bull's-eyes on both of your backs.

Do you want to keep looking over your shoulder, or do you want to keep cashing those nice paychecks with a little something left over?

Tip 13: Don't Go Down with the Ship

Alex had a very decent job, paying him in the low six figures. He sold business opportunities for a firm that had a genius at the helm. The founder was masterful at direct-mail marketing, so the sales crew usually had plentiful inquires to convert into clients.

Alex was thrilled, because the economy was troubled, and good jobs were scarce. Having cycled through some terrible posts, he felt this one was a keeper.

Cozy as the situation was, storm clouds could be seen outside of Alex's picture window. Customer satisfaction was a growing concern. A very high proportion of clients felt they made a mistake when they invested in the opportunities that were being sold. Many wanted refunds, and some purchasers posted their concerns online.

Alex began noticing that an increasing proportion of his new sales kicked out, and these required "saving." Sellers were charged by the company to save deals. A special unit that operated on commissions was given the task of retaining customers that threatened to cancel.

The company's Better Business Bureau rating plummeted. This fact was publicized on the Internet, making once-eager inquiries into suspicious fence-sitters that couldn't be reached with a follow-up call.

It was becoming clear to Alex that the company's eroding reputation was going to put it out of business, if not right away, then within a matter of months. Yet he was still making more money there than he could make at any other opportunity he had investigated.

Should he have quit? Or should he have stayed and gone down with the ship?

In his case, the answer became clear when the ultimate strength of the company, its direct-marketing capability, started to weaken. The phones weren't ringing off the hook, as they had been known to do on a predictable and reliable basis. Clearly, Alex thought, the time was coming when the doors would be shuttered.

He quit, and fairly quickly he found another position that didn't pay quite as well.

His previous company was able to remain in business for a full year after Alex left the scene. So as it turned out, he could have hung in there, squeezing out an income. Was he right to leave?

I think so.

The problem with an employment vessel that has sprung a leak is that it produces fear in salespeople. Fear, for all practical purposes, is toxic to sellers because it erodes confidence, a necessary ingredient in successful selling.

Prospects can sense when sellers are committed to their firm, and they can also detect when people sound like they're temps. Savvy buyers will often ask salespeople, "How long have you been working there?"

"I just joined the company" is not the reply they want to get.

There is also a stigma associated with having worked for companies that failed and for firms that are famous for achieving customer dissatisfaction. You don't want to say to a prospective boss, "Oh, my last company went out of business," because some of that taint will rub off on you.

Leave while you can, and it is better to do so earlier than later.

Tip #14: Don't Hitch Your Wagon to a Failing Industry

One of the most desirable aspects of working for other people is that you can choose the industry in which you're going to work. You can choose the location—in the middle of metropolis or in the outback. And of course, you can choose specific companies, though we often fail to see this fact.

When we're job hunting, a fixed menu is presented to us. On the menu are companies that are running ads for salespeople. So it would seem that they are choosing us, correct?

Not so. Nothing is to stop you from pitching companies on using your services.

What you do NOT want to do is to seek work or stay in the employment of a company or industry that is failing or overpopulated.

An example or two will be helpful. A few years ago it became apparent to me that writing books for conventional publishers was becoming a riskier proposition. In the space of a few years, many of my publishers merged or were sold to other firms. Editors were displaced, and the marketing staffs were curtailed. Because of the Internet, bookstores were closing, so there were fewer outlets through which sales could be made. Ebooks had not yet matured into viable platforms. Advances paid to authors by traditional publishers were plummeting.

I was in negotiations with one house that wanted a book I had written. I didn't like the advance, and I felt that channeling my book through them would result in disappointing sales.

So I elected to record the program as an audio first. I received a larger advance, and sales were brisk. It became a very successful venture for me. I went on to record more programs, with success.

But it was crucial that I stopped to take stock of the diminishing fortunes of traditional publishing. I had already paid a price by expecting this industry to deliver to me the good profits and prospects that it once did. In fact, I should have seen the writing on the wall years before I did.

Right now, another field is being rocked by technological change: the energy sector. Fracking and shale-extraction methods are bringing down the price of oil.

Solar, wind, and other alternative energy sources are becoming cheaper and more popular. In a word, I would *not* enter the oil business today.

Are there jobs? Of course. Oil is too big not to need people. But in an atmosphere of diminishing profits, sales commissions have to be thinning, as do the ranks of sellers.

You've heard the joke, "Would the last one here please turn out the lights?" You don't want to be that person in a given company or industry.

Recently, it became clear that Congress was concerned about the high level of student-loan defaults that has beset the country. Among those with some of the largest debts were former attendees of vocational schools. Many of these people were frustrated that they were saddled with huge debt payments, yet they were unable to secure jobs in the fields for which they had trained. It was clear that legislatures would place pressures and restrictions upon vocational schools. With federally insured loans harder to get, fewer students would enroll. This meant the vocational-school sector would shrink.

In this atmosphere, who would want to teach or to sell in this field? Go where profits are strong, where there are good margins, and where there is relatively little competition. This means working for opportunistic firms. Generally, they will be relatively new on the scene, and they'll be selling something unique.

A quick example: I consulted for a company that manufactured and sold gift-wrapping supplies. Their specialty was wrapping with people's names on them, like "Chad" and "Bill" and "Megan." As far as I knew, this company had the field pretty much to itself. It was able to charge big prices, and its salespeople prospered. While the printing presses were fairly sophisticated, this was not a technology-driven entity. It was a niche player, and it owned its competitive space. As I recall, this company had about 150 employees. It was relatively small.

I think you'll find there are a lot of firms like this one. As long as they are profitable and they have a competitive advantage without cutthroat competition, they are the sort of firm for which you should want to sell.

Tip 15: Don't Press

When I was going through a batting slump, my dad would say, "Don't press."

I didn't have a clue to what he meant. But he saw something in my demeanor that he felt was keeping me from hitting. Now, decades later, I suspect he had a point.

I was stressing about whether I'd succeed at the plate. I was tense. I wasn't at all relaxed.

Later I'd study martial arts, earn a black belt, and instruct others. I would teach them this lesson: to relax— to *not* try to muscle their way to effectiveness.

In any sport, and in selling, you can simply try too hard.

In sports, when you try to hit a ball with all of your strength, you're setting yourself up for failure. Most times, the ball will travel a shorter distance than it would have gone without so much effort. Or you'll swing and miss. One set of muscles will be doing the right thing: attempting to hit the ball. But an extra set of muscles will be brought into play—harmfully—from the excess exertion. This second set will be working against the first set and will be slowing you down. It's like pushing and pulling at the same time.

If you relax and don't try so hard, your swing or your punch or kick will be faster. In many cases, you'll be expressing even more power without all of the debilitating effort.

Time and again, I've seen this happen in sales. Recently, when I was testing a presentation for a consulting client, I executed the basics very well with a prospect. I calmly explained that I was going to be sending him an agreement and that he needed to sign and return it right away.

At that place of business, most sales resulted only after repeated efforts to close the order were made. This process took two to four weeks.

My initial prospect returned the paperwork in three days, and it became the largest sale in the company's history.

I told everyone I believe in taking the most direct path to a yes. That's what I did.

Some of my sales took longer to make, and this did usher in some stress, which made me press. But I was aware of this trap, so I talked things over with myself.

Pressing can be caused internally or externally.

Sales managers, who are well meaning and generally rational individuals, will push their staff to try harder.

This means working longer shifts, taking work home on evenings and weekends, and even keeping up their customer contacts during vacations.

These efforts seem to make sense. "Work more and sell more!"—correct? But this is misguided. Each seller has a sweet spot, an ideal level of exertion. If that threshold isn't reached, he or she won't reach full potential. If that level of ideal exertion is greatly surpassed, effectiveness will diminish. The seller will become exhausted and will not be able to summon enough energy to do well.

Listlessness comes across to prospects as indifference. It also is the farthest imaginable demeanor from enthusiasm.

Don't try to earn an A for effort. Effort, if it becomes pressing beyond a certain point, boomerangs, preventing us from reaching our sales potential.

Tip 16: Don't Be the Salesperson Who Knew Too Much

Legend tells us there was a fellow in the early 1900s who had no real skills but who aspired to doing great things. Scouring the employment listings, he came across an opportunity for a harmonica salesman.

Knowing less about music than most other things, he was reluctant to apply. But his stomach grumbled, and the rent had to be paid. So he overcame his trepidation and sought an interview.

He was hired, and after the briefest possible training program he was put into the field, knocking on doors.

At the end of his first week, he had made more money than anyone he knew inside or outside of his family. In fact, he had set a companywide record for the most harmonicas sold in a week.

As you can imagine, he was elated. He couldn't wait for Monday morning to arrive. That would be his opportunity to speak to people who could reveal even more to him about the features of the great product he sold so well.

He went from department to department. "What else can you tell me about this harmonica?" he pleaded.

Almost every person he spoke to shrugged and said, "I'm sure you know more about this harmonica than I do!"

Deflated, he was about to abandon his inquiry. But he had one more door to knock on. The sign on the front said, "Engineering."

"Great," he thought. "I'll talk to the person who designed it."

"I can only tell you one thing that you don't already know," the fellow in the lab coat said. "The harmonica only plays in one key." He went on to explain what that limitation meant in practical terms.

I wish I could say the story had a happy ending. But I can't, because that would be a lie. The salesperson never made as many harmonica sales as he did in his first week.

Aren't we supposed to get better as we gain experience? Shouldn't increases in product knowledge assist us in selling more items?

Yes, this is the way selling *should* work, but it doesn't.

This tale stands for the proposition that salespeople can know too much about their goods and services. Sadly, the more they know, the more they feel they have to disclose what they know to everyone, even if these details aren't requested.

Our harmonica seller pitched only one thing during his first week in the business: harmonicas make nice music. After learning what he did, he felt duty-bound to say that this device had a limitation: it could play in a single key only. Pointing out that drawback lost sales, and he lost confidence.

If you haven't heard this before, let me be the first to do you the favor: product knowledge is vastly overrated! If you can, learn enough to make sales, and learn no more. Limit what you say. And don't give prospects reasons NOT to buy.

Don't be the salesperson who knew too much!

Tip 17: Develop High Frustration Tolerance

Can't wait for that prospect to get back to you as she promised to do? Feel antsy whenever a deal doesn't come together immediately? Hate it when you have to catch up on paperwork or when suddenly a deal seems to be stalled because of a holiday?

These are typical frustrations that everyone encounters in selling. But some of us "awfulize" about them. We grow angry, bitter, and fly off the handle when everything doesn't go exactly our way, especially when we've experienced a recent round of robust success. We expect every deal to come together just right, and when they don't, we wail.

These are symptoms of low frustration tolerance, or LFT, as psychologists label it. Children suffer from it. They expect instant gratification. They want dessert *now*!

In selling, sometimes we actually get what we want on the spot. This spoils us for those times when we have to show patience, or high frustration tolerance.

One of the last things we learn as we mature is the value of patience. Sadly, our insistence on instant results can cost us a fortune in sales. Many sellers, and their managers, push relentlessly for an immediate yes or no from prospects.

I'm not speaking of closing. I'm referring to the attempt to seal deals that cannot yet come together. Would you rather push a prospect into saying no now, just to end the suspense, than wait for time to pass?

If you develop high frustration tolerance, you'll be willing to ease up, let go on occasion, and allow nature to take its course.

Providing some prospects with breathing room can be a great closing technique in itself. Today's prospects are very sensitive about being pushed into decisions. Fearing they're being hustled, many folks will run from us, sensing that we're trying to rush them into making a bad decision.

Appreciate that these people exist. One way of demonstrating your character is by purposely allowing them some distance. This doesn't mean you should fail to follow up. It simply means don't go nuts or make catastrophic errors because you have an irrational need for closure.

If you seem too eager to get a sale, believe me, that sale will elude you. It's OK to want it and to do all of those things necessary to earn it, but don't want it so much that it shows.

If you're in sales, frustration comes with the territory. Tolerating it is a skill that we have to develop. Once we do, our paychecks will be fatter and our blood pressure will be lower.

Tip 18: Get Back to the Basics and Thrive

Salespeople shoot themselves in the wallet by making the process more complicated than it needs to be.

You know what I'm talking about. Let's say you're being trained for a new job. Typically, you'll be guided through a presentation, or you'll do a ride-along or a desk drive with an experienced rep to see and hear how she does it.

Good so far, right? You're learning the essentials. But if your training program lasts too long, you'll run the risk of becoming overwhelmed with details, most of which you'll never remember when you start selling on your own.

I've noticed an inverse correlation between how long a sales training program lasts and its effectiveness in giving recruits what they need to succeed.

I'll give you an example. I was brought in to consult to a major mutual-fund company that had a six-week training program in place. Reps had to wait that long to get on the phones and sell investment products.

Having come from a very different corporate sales background, I found that way too long to wait before selling. When I was coming up at Time-Life, we had a four-hour training program. This included a briefing on the products and the sales methodology. We knew who would succeed and who would fail with a 95 percent certainty after the initial four-hour shift had concluded. In those cases where we were uncertain, we invited them to come back for a second four-hour shift the next day.

So to me, six weeks at the mutual-fund company seemed like forever. What I did was insist that the trainers train me over the course of six days, not six weeks. They protested, saying they could never fit all of the information in, but they did. Even in that truncated session, there was still a tremendous amount of fluff and trivia.

I cut the six days back to three. Trainees ended up being more effective much faster.

Plus, they focused more and their anxieties were reduced, because they sprang into action sooner rather than later.

When you have succeeded in a sales job, you also arrive at a point of potentially endless embellishment. You start including everything you know into your presentations. You answer questions that haven't been raised by prospects, just in case they're thinking about them. In a word, you hopelessly overcomplicate your presentations. Your sales decline and you fall into a deep slump. It seems as if you can't buy a sale.

At wits' end, you ask your manager to observe you, and you're shocked to hear, "Gary, you're way off the presentation! Get back on it."

You heed the counsel, and suddenly you're making sales again, just as new trainees do!

Most presentations have been designed to provide you with the shortest possible path to a yes. This is critical as a time- and energy-management tool. Anything that doesn't contribute to a sale, that overcomplicates the process, must be jettisoned.

Regularly monitor your own presentations. What have you inserted that simply doesn't belong there?

Cast it out.

Tip 19: Stay Employed!

As a breed, salespeople are opportunistic. We're always looking for a bigger and better deal. There's nothing wrong with this, if we don't hop, skip, and jump from one position to another.

The problem isn't that sellers make poor money when we're selling. The problem is we don't get enough actual selling time—talking to people who can buy.

Part of this challenge results from a lack of leads. Another aspect of the problem is poor time management, placing clerical tasks and distractions ahead of communications with buyers.

But a huge miscue is to permit sizeable gaps in your employment. Ideally, you should always be on at least one company's payroll.

This means job hunting and working at the same time. It's not easy, but some of the best employers cast a wary eye at unemployed salespeople. "If she's so good, why isn't she selling right now?" is the question that pops into mind.

When you shop jobs and are employed at the same time, you're more desirable, especially if you can claim that you are number one or two on the team.

Plus, you have a great BATNA. Negotiators know this term. It stands for *best alternative to a negotiated agreement*.

Translated, BATNA asks, "What are you going to do if the new employer won't pay you enough, or you simply don't like each other?"

That's easy with a suitable BATNA. You'll keep your current position. After all, you're making a living when you're employed.

You might be able to insist on a signing bonus with a new firm, because you'll be forgoing income and commissions that are captive in the pipeline at the old place. Above all, you'll have role distance, which is a take-it-or-leave-it attitude when you job-hunt.

But perhaps the most important reason to stay employed is that downtime I mentioned before. It is very costly to have interruptions in your income. Missing a few months or even a few weeks of pay can ruin your overall earnings for the year. Plus, you may have to incur debt to stay afloat. Living on charge cards can cost you 30 percent in interest alone, and recapturing that, plus paying back the principal of the loan in a new job, will be difficult.

We all get antsy from time to time. No one likes to feel underpaid. But even if you aren't earning big bucks right now, it still beats nothing.

If you can, try to steal second base while keeping your foot on first.

Tip 20: Use a Bigger Voice

As a breed, salespeople are known for being outgoing and even the life of the party. We tell jokes and generally have a good time. So this tip may not apply to you if you're already in the sales field, unless your order volume has taken a dip.

If sellers are allowed to sound too introverted, which is to say if their voices dip below a certain threshold of audibility, they simply won't sell as well as a person with a louder voice.

We first detected this correlation when I was working for Time-Life. As a manager, if I entered the room and you could hear a pin drop, I knew our sales had slipped as well. Shyness and selling don't go together.

In a quiet room, I'd bellow, "Get your voices UP!" Immediately the team would comply, and orders shot up as well.

In fairness, if you've been ill, or if you have laryngitis, you may not feel like ratcheting up the volume, or possibly you cannot. I understand, but your sales will suffer.

Higher volume creates an aura of confidence. A big voice sends a metamessage. It says, "I believe in what I'm doing" and "I really mean it!"

Lower volumes contradict these impressions. They signal insecurity, and prospects will mirror that attitude, recoiling from the offer instead of embracing it.

Monitor yourself for volume level. You'll find you are most susceptible to unconsciously lowering your volume when you've gone for some time without earning a sale. This will necessitate artificially building it back up to a higher level.

How do you accomplish that? Take deeper breaths and use your diaphragm to push out your words. When you get your voice-producing musculature working correctly, the bigger voice will come forth. Suddenly you'll be selling again, and you won't need the extra stimulus. Until then, fake it until you make it!

But you can sound too loud, correct? True, yet if you had to choose between sounding too soft or too loud, generally louder would be better. Unless you're selling to librarians, that is!

Tip 21: Don't Stereotype Your Prospects!

I worked my way through undergraduate school with Time-Life and at other jobs. When I graduated at twenty-one, I was hired as an account executive at an upscale Beverly Hills car-leasing company.

On one particularly slow afternoon, an eighteen-year-old came into the office accompanied by his girlfriend. It was my turn to handle walk-ins, so they were my prospects.

I asked him what he was looking for, and he replied that he wanted a Ferrari.

"Doesn't everyone!" I thought to myself.

I assumed this kid was dreaming. How could this poorly attired, baby-faced imp afford a ride like that? No way did he have means to make his wish come true.

I told him he'd need to fill out an application, which he did. I don't recall that he had any credit references.

Dismissively, I said, "We'll call you once your application is processed," and with those words he and his mate left the premises.

I was doing more pressing things, like paperwork, when the normally sour credit manager bounded into my cubicle like a carefree gazelle.

"Where is your customer?" he asked brightly.

"He left," I responded.

"He left? Lease him *anything* he wants. He's a trust-fund baby!"

This meant that for all practical purposes, the kid was loaded. He didn't need a long credit history. He had enough bucks available to drive what he wanted.

Excitedly, I got on the phone, but I couldn't track him down.

The next day he answered my call with a chilly tone.

"You've been approved!" I announced with some residue of surprise in my voice.

"That's OK," he said sharply. "I bought two Ferraris at the dealership on Wilshire, one for me and one for my girlfriend."

I would have made a huge commission if I had earned the sale, but here I was, stunned by what had taken place.

It took some time for me to tease out the truth of what had transpired. Finally I realized my error, and it was a typical mistake that every seller has made. A certain prospect doesn't fit our mental image of the typical or the most desirable buyer. We succumb to the false belief that the person isn't worth our best efforts to pursue, because a sale "probably" won't be made.

Why waste time? We blow them off, or we cut corners. We may even hand them off to someone else.

If we're lucky, we'll learn about our mistakes and have a chance to reform ourselves. In most cases, however, we'll never find out how and with whom we blew it, because they'll disappear without a word and avoid our efforts at further contact.

We never really know who will or who won't buy until we have gone through the process with them.

Don't qualify your prospects' motivations too harshly, as I did. And avoid stereotyping them, because you'll find there are always people that buy whom we have written off.

Be kind enough and thorough enough so they'll buy from you!

Tip 22: Do the Math of Success in the Sales Job Interview

It's typical of salespeople to be optimistic. We have a can-do attitude. Like the Navy's Seabees, we think we can build sales anywhere, anytime, and under the worst of conditions. Heck, we thrive on adversity! So when we go into an interview, we put our best foot forward and project an unshakeable sense of self-confidence.

All of these things are good, but the same optimism and grandiosity are coming from the other side of the table. They're presenting the sales opportunity in the most favorable light. They're also painting a super-rosy portrait of what your sales progress will be on the job. The more they want you, the more they'll bend, twist, and mutilate the truth to make it conform to what will appear to be the ideal sales job.

Once it has been established that they want you and you can do the job, it is time to do what I call the *math of success*. You can do this exercise first do in your head, silently, and then with the hiring authority.

Imagine they say you can earn $100K in commissions on top of a $40K base that they provide.

You should be armed with several questions:

On average, how long does it take to get to the $100K level? And to $50K, and to $25K?

How many people are at the $100K level now? How long did it take them to arrive at this point?

How many sales per day, week, or month does it take to reach $100K?

What's the average commission value of a sale?

Out of every ten presentations, how many result in a sale?

Let's examine the purpose of these questions, for example, *how long does it take to see serious money rolling in?* How much money do you have in savings? How long can you subsidize this job until it pays for itself?

If they say you can expect to reach $100K by the end of year two, forget it. That's a long, long time in the future. Even saying that you'll reach that performance level at the end of the first year will give you the wrong impression.

This timeline makes it sound as if you'll be steadily garnering $8,333 per month in commission pay all the way to the one-year point. That's very unlikely.

More likely is struggling for a month or two and bringing in nothing or close to nothing. Then, if you catch on, you might start climbing the rungs of achievement after that.

Whatever they say, you can at least DOUBLE how long it will take to reach a given sales goal. You can also cut in half or by two-thirds the amount of commission they predict you'll earn.

I'm not saying everybody lies. I'm saying sales managers and business brass bend the facts to suit the circumstances. And in this circumstance, they're selling YOU!

Tip 23: Bargain for the Highest Possible Salary

I mentioned the salesman who earned a million-dollar commission on his first deal. I also pointed out that until he accomplished it, he had earned zero sales and zero money on that job, because it paid a straight commission.

If working on a straight commission plan makes you tingle with excitement while keeping you focused, then of course find an opportunity that pays you that way. But I would guess that 95 percent of salespeople do not thrive under this sort of all-or-nothing, feast-or-famine pay plan. Indeed, most find it stress-inducing and even overwhelming. If you're busy envisioning calamities such as starvation for you and your family, you're not going to have the right energy or vibe to sell.

The alternative is arranging a set amount of income that is guaranteed. Typically, this will take one of two forms: a draw against commissions or a salary.

A draw provides a definite amount of money each pay period. At the end of the pay period, your commissions are tallied. If the total commission is greater in value than the draw you were paid, you'll receive additional money for the surplus. If the total commission is less, you'll be in the hole. Technically, you'll owe the company the difference.

Some firms will dock your future commissions to make up for their overpayments to you. At other firms, the deal is reset for the next pay period, and you pay back nothing. If an underachieving trend continues, and period after period you fall short—that is, your earnings don't cover the draw—you'll probably be shown the door.

A salary operates differently. You're paid a definite amount, irrespective of how much you sell. You may also earn a commission on each order or after an established number of orders is reached. In the final analysis, you will still have to produce to keep your job.

However, the psychology and practical value of the two plans are very different.

When paid a salary, you are being given a stipend for dedicating your time and talents to the task. In a sense, you're being paid to try, to exert a professional effort. A salary also acknowledges that you have bills to pay. Your landlord or mortgage holder and car financier won't accept conditional compensation. They bargained for a certain amount each and every billing interval.

But I believe the most significant aspect of a salary for the seller is that it shifts the risks of failure to the company. For example, let's say a new competitor enters the field, and it is offering such low pricing that it is gobbling up huge chunks of market share.

As a seller, you may or may not be empowered to cut your prices. But it's clear that the new competitor's low-ball pricing is going to cost you sales or seriously impair your commissions.

Who should bear the brunt of such market upheavals? Who is in the better position to anticipate and to ride out such a market disturbance?

From my view, it is the company. It should have plans in place to tide itself and its employees over until it can cope with the sudden sea change. If you own or manage a business, tumult is to be expected. Nothing stands still.

Not only should sellers be paid a salary, but they should bargain for the largest possible salary they can get. The proportion of fixed to variable pay should be as high as it can be while still leaving room for incentive pay based on superior performance.

Let me give you an example. An employer I consulted for set up the following compensation plan for sellers:

Plan A: You could earn a 50 percent commission on each order.

Plan B: You could earn $2000 per week as a salary and a 25 percent commission on each order.

The math of success that I described earlier established that it was possible to succeed either way.

An experienced seller was hired in the middle of October. He realized that the holiday season was rapidly approaching when he came aboard. Because he was not in retail, where sales can be expected to peak, he predicted the opposite was more likely to occur. People would delay in buying the services he was selling. Plus, he inferred that fewer leads would be provided, because the company would be reluctant to purchase prospects that could not be expected to instantly become clients. So a downturn in sales activity could be expected to persist well into January or February, because there would be fewer deals to close in the pipeline. Because of these facts, he opted for the salary plus 25 percent commission rate.

How did he come out after three months? His total compensation was approximately 53 percent of each dollar brought in, and the company's take was 47 percent. So the seller came out at least slightly ahead, correct?

Financially, this is true. But he also came out emotionally. Instead of stressing over whether sales would be made during the holiday lull, he focused on earning the orders that he could. Had he stressed out, he would have pressed too hard for sales, and he probably would not have achieved at the high level that he ended up reaching.

In this case, the salary plus commission benefited both the seller and firm, and I would argue that that is most often the case, providing sellers are capable and the math of success portends success.

Companies, however, often maintain a different view. They assert that it is human nature to slacken if one earns a guaranteed income, and to slacken to limpness if that guaranteed salary is high. Sellers need to be tense, to be on their toes, to be and to stay hungry, I often hear such employers maintain.

I believe that with such attitudes and practices, they are setting themselves and their salespeople up for failure.

I should note one more thing. When you're being paid a good salary, come what may, companies are incentivized to provide you with the tools of success. They don't want you to be idle, so typically they'll keep giving you sufficient leads to call on and other forms of support. If it costs them nothing to make you idle, all too often they'll choose to starve you.

Make them do the right thing! Bargain for the biggest salary you can get.

Don't worry. You'll justify it!

Tip 24: Don't Spend Your Commissions before You Earn Them

I used to joke that I wasn't any good at math until dollar signs were attached to the numbers.

This is partly true. I've always enjoyed estimating how much money I was about to make. "If I do this and that, I'll earn X amount!"

It's fun to conjecture about income, especially when you first start seeing the sales come in. It's also practical to know that you'll need to speak to a hundred people each day, week, or month to arrive at your sales and income goals. Planning your work and then working your plan are essential to getting on track and staying on track.

But don't count your chickens before they hatch. Never assume that certain prospects are definite buyers, that there's no way you can lose their business or fail to see the commission they represent land in your paycheck. Above all, don't change your lifestyle, incurring large debts or making major expenditures on speculation.

I've been fortunate to earn large amounts of money in bursts. Usually these infusions of cash have come to me after I've done some concerted sales and marketing work.

When the checks are coming in like a huge tide, you can easily convince yourself that you'll always be drenched in income. You forget the dry spells and especially the efforts that it took to just keep your head above water.

This is dangerous, because it is common to buy a superexpensive car or to rent or to buy more house than you need when things are going well. You end up spending your commissions before they're earned, and this is always perilous.

But this is what many of your sales managers will nudge you to do.

Their theory is simple. If you want to make great salespeople from average ones, just put them into debt!

Then they'll hustle and constantly think wolves are at the door.

In a very real sense, they will be. If you've overspent, you're going to be in the worst shape to fend them off.

I'm fond of a comment in Sun Tzu's famous book of strategy *The Art of War:* "Victory with exhaustion means defeat in the battle to come."

To apply this to your monthly overhead, if you struggle to finance that new car or home or fancy vacation, you'll run the risk of not having the energy to meet the recurring payment obligations.

Plus, companies are not as reliable as they were a few decades ago. For decades, even the largest firms operated by a code of honor. They'd pay their employees and vendors even if they took their good time about it.

But today you may be working for a start-up that faces long odds of succeeding. You can't afford to count on firms such as these to meet their payrolls. They always seem cash-starved and on the brink of extinction.

This is tricky psychologically. You should be hoping for the best and planning for the worst. We should have a positive outlook about our ability to produce sales and to improve, and we need to believe in our associates and our companies. But we can't forget that highs and lows happen, and it's always important to have a reserve of cash, a cushion that can give you a soft landing if you experience temporary turbulence.

Don't spend tomorrow's hoped-for income today. As career counselors advise, have at least three to six months' worth of monthly expenditures saved up.

Make this your goal, so down the line you can splurge here and there.

Tip 25: Don't Gossip about Clients and Prospects

I was gearing up to deliver a major keynote speech in Las Vegas to a meeting of an international home-furnishings company. I was proud of the fact that I was the headliner, the main attraction. I love large audiences because they get the adrenalin going. My program would be attended by 400 people.

In the meantime, I was hustling for more business. Speaking to a fellow named Don about promoting my speeches to his client base, I let it slip that I was doing this association's Vegas convention the following week.

"They're one of my clients!" he said, with some irritation in his voice.

"Small world!" I replied, thinking that my engagement with them was proof that I was a major-league speaker that he would be wise to affiliate with.

He went on to ask me about my theme for the talk. Feeling flattered, I told him and noted some of the key points that I'd be covering. We ended our chat, and I didn't give another thought to it.

Arriving at the convention in Vegas, I noted the association had added a speaker. Who was it? It was Don's clone, a contract speaker he sent out to do those events that couldn't afford him. His topic actually mirrored mine!

He went on right before me, and he did his best to steal all of my thunder. He covered the same points I had disclosed to Don.

I was in a state of shock. Even if I was going to offer a unique twist to the topic, I was repeating the material. People would get bored. They'd walk out into the casino to gamble. They'd talk among themselves—rude behavior that I can't stand in an audience.

In fact, this is pretty much what happened.

I discovered that Don got on the phone immediately after I had spoken with him and made a special deal with the association to provide the clone at a deeply discounted rate.

For me, although I was paid, the event was a flop. I never worked for that association again. And I didn't get any work from Don. At that point, I felt he was not the sort of chap I wanted or needed to consort with anyway.

My point is simple: don't gossip about your clients!

Gossip can shoot you in the wallet in another way. Imagine you're making calls from a bullpen, and you stop after every conversation. Turning to your right or left, you insist on sharing the contents of what was just said on the prior call. That's gossiping about your clients. It not only wastes your time, it prevents you from making the next call, and it prevents your associates from doing their work.

Plus, by sharing details with your peers, you're tempting the fates. They might try to steal those accounts from you.

Before you reply that there's no way this can happen, believe me, it can. They can have the account reassigned to them on the grounds that you complained about having to deal with that contact person. Or your pal could say you seemed out of your league, and he could do a better job.

Maybe this sounds like paranoia to you, but believe me, it pays to keep certain details about clients and prospects completely confidential.

Tip 26: Save Your Energy and Avoid Energy Vampires

There are a million distractions you can succumb to if you're not vigilant.

You can engage in gossip. You can play company politics. You can get too embroiled in the agony and ecstasy of your local sports teams. You can bring your worries to work—that you won't make this month's car payment or housing tab or your kid's tuition bill. You can be plagued by regrets, kicking yourself for not buying that winning lottery ticket, or for dropping out of school.

One guy I knew beat himself up every day of his stunted career after having quit a job at a Silicon Valley start-up that became an international giant in the software field. He was the fifth person hired, and the first to take a walk. Had he stayed a little while longer, he would have been given stock options worth millions.

Everyone has regrets. I've turned down lots of deals that in hindsight would have been a net plus. I describe some of these miscues in my book *Dr. Gary S. Goodman's 77 Best Practices in Negotiation.*

But all of these issues and ruminations have to be left at the door each day as we start to sell. Obviously, if you're worrying, or regretting, or engaging in aimless and needless small talk, you'll waste time. Time is money.

Equally importantly, you'll waste your energy. Energy is always a finite resource. I know a very seasoned entrepreneur in the investment business who believes a seller can only make five decent presentations a day. If you try to beat this quota, you'll run out of gas. Your figure could be higher or lower, but suffice it to say you have a limit, and so do I.

We're not getting paid when we're looking into the rearview mirror. In fact, anything that keeps us out of present-moment consciousness, the NOW TIME of selling, will sap our energy and torpedo our earnings.

Our neighbors at work, the folks in the next office or cube, can be energy vampires. Some of them feed off the energy they cause us to dissipate. Our loss is their gain.

I take frequent stretch breaks when I feel my energy is waning. I also leave the office and take quarter- to half-mile walks around the area. This is good in a number of ways. It contributes to fitness. It interrupts stinking thinking. It gets you away from bad influences, human and environmental.

If you want a practical test that will reveal who is an energy vampire and who is normal, ask yourself, "How do I feel after I am in this person's presence, or after I get off a call, or finish an email exchange with them?"

If you're wasted, then you'll have your answer.

It gets somewhat trickier if the vampire is your boss, but the same advice applies. Avoid managers that leave you feeling drained. See if you can work remotely, from home or a satellite office. Ask to move your desk out of the path of this voltage-zapper. If it's impossible to avoid the person, try to Zen out if the person is criticizing you or talking your ear off. If these tactics don't work, find another place to ply your trade.

Time is money, but energy is money as well.

Tip 27: Always Swing a Lead Bat

When I was playing baseball, we used to take warm-up swings with an extra heavy bat. By the time we picked up our standard hitting device, it felt superlight. In theory, that meant we would be able swing fast enough to crush the fastest fastball.

At least it felt that way, and the process of taking heavy practice swings in the on-deck circle gave me confidence to face the meanest pitchers.

I think the same principle applies to selling. By dealing with some of the most difficult prospects and buyers, we develop the capacity to master routine encounters.

Let's say you have been trying to close a fence-sitter, someone who won't make a decision in a timely way.

You've followed up a dozen times, and you've made what seems like absolutely zero progress.

There may be a good reason to abandon this relationship and to move on to someone more receptive. As long as you have another prospect that is more malleable, it could make sense.

But the lead-bat theory says adversity makes you strong. By pushing against an immovable object, you're doing sales isometrics. It builds muscles. When you get fresh leads or you sense you can close someone, you'll be a tiger, springing into action and seizing the prize.

In a sense, there is no such thing as losing a sale, or even not making one. There is selling successfully and muscle building. If you're not doing one, you're doing the other.

For example, I dealt with a fence-sitter who couldn't cost-justify giving me the order. I answered every objection. I showed him how he could be paying a lot more elsewhere for the same item. I joked with him. Finally, I even said he wouldn't invest the kind of time with his prospects that I invested with him. All of which was calculated to get him to make a decision, even a negative one, if there was no hope left of earning his business.

That's the way things turned out. Instead of telling myself I wasted my time, I patted myself on the back. I hung in there with him a lot longer than many would have done. I tried new ways to get an order.

I built sales muscles!

So don't avoid difficult prospects or eschew adversity. Swing a lead bat. You may find there's gold in it.

Tip 28: If They Envy You, They Won't Buy From You!

I had a career in the vacuum-cleaner sales business. It lasted for all of one day, but it made a permanent impression.

I was training with an experienced seller who drove to work in a new Cadillac. I started to walk up to the passenger door to get in when he stopped me. "No, we're taking *that* car," he said, pointing to an old white station wagon that had enough miles on it to have gone to the moon.

This guy set a new standard in frumpiness. His slacks were shiny, his sports jacket rumpled, and he seemed as if he may have squinted sunrise from the door of a tavern. But he was their top seller, so this first day in the business would be spent with him.

"Don't say anything," the manager warned. "Just observe him."

Everything about the gent I was shadowing seemed pathetic, especially how he greeted homemakers after they answered their doorbells.

He smiled crookedly, and then mumbled something about how he'd like to vacuum their living rooms for free.

Surprisingly, they responded, I believe out of pity.

He vacuumed the rooms and then opened the machine and emptied the dirt-filled bag onto the center of their now-pristine carpet.

"Oh, gosh!" the homemakers would cry out.

"Did you realize there was so much dirt embedded in your carpet?"

"Of course not!"

"You don't want to keep living this way, do you?" he'd ask.

"No."

Within a few minutes he'd write up the order.

Quickly I realized that his entire presentation and even his frumpy, pathetic, pitiable demeanor were very carefully orchestrated and rehearsed. In real life, back at the office, he was anything but modest and unassuming. Instead of crouching and looking up at prospects, he stood erect and lorded it over everyone.

It was time to get back in his Cadillac and drive home to the gated community in which he lived. He realized something that I'm going to share with you.

Never come across as superior to your prospects. Allow them to feel in some ways superior to you.

For example, I live in one of the most temperate climates in the world. When I call certain regions that are blanketed with snow, I tell them how much I miss the seasons. This is true, but it isn't the kind of wistfulness that will get me to move back.

In late August and September, I'll ask, "Have the leaves started to turn yet?" They are beautiful, and on my computer I have screen savers with autumnal foliage displayed during that time, and winter scenes later on.

Wherever my prospects are, it is ALWAYS BETTER than where I am! That's a rule.

Don't get spoiled by your success, and don't compete with your clients. Make the right impression. Drive up in the beater. Drive home in the luxury car.

Tip 29: Take the Fastest Path to a YES!

When I was starting out as a full-time consultant, I decided to offer seminars through universities. These were aimed at businesspeople, and I chose universities as my distributors for several reasons.

They are generally credible institutions. I held advanced academic credentials, including an earned doctorate. I had been teaching undergraduates for five years, so I was comfortable inside ivy walls. And they had money and a marketing platform.

The key was to convince the right people to say yes to sponsoring my seminar.

Knowing academics, and the scholastic sensibility, I realized a typical sales approach that seemed too strategic would backfire. After a lot of thought, I determined that I had to seem guileless, absolutely straightforward, but not lacking confidence in my course or my authority to present it and present it well.

Here's pretty much what I said when the call screeners had put me through to the decision makers:

"I teach at DePauw University, and I've developed a one-day workshop for businesspeople, and I was wondering what we might do to pursue the prospect of offering it through your university."

And I silenced myself.

Typically, I'd hear these questions:

Do you have any written materials you can send me?

Have you conducted it before?

What did you charge?

How many people signed up?

What's your fee?

When would you like to present it here?

Please go back to what I said to open the conversation. With regard to the frequently asked questions, I could have covered all this information up front, yes? Purposely, I left it out, because I wanted to take the most direct path to a yes. The way to do this was to be very sparing in my sales talk, while stimulating these prospects to sell themselves. Fundamentally, I asked how to offer the class and not "may we?" I needed direction, not permission. I assumed we would be doing the class.

That's a part of streamlined selling. It's almost like saying, "Ready or not, here I come!" But it is delivered in an ultracalm, nonthreatening, fact-finding manner.

Sellers shoot themselves in the wallet by trying to answer everything *before* prospects bring up these points or concerns. That's wasteful, and it plants the seeds of objections. It presumes resistance, and thus causes it.

I'll bet your entire persuasive message could be boiled down to a sentence or two. Have you ever tried to do that, to distill it? It is worth a ton of money to you. You'll save time and effort. You'll get to the bottom line. And you'll let buyers help you to get a YES out of them.

Plus, for what it's worth, you won't sound like an over-the-top pitchman.

Eliminate the unnecessary. If you insert too much fluff, the going will be rough.

Tip 30: The Deal Isn't Made Until the Money Is Paid

It wasn't until later in my sales career that I heard the adage "Buyers are liars."

The first time this was mentioned, I cringed. I never saw them this way. I've faced tough bargainers and people that played possum and were hard to reach. I've been stalled and have fielded countless excuses. But I didn't consider buyers to be liars, certainly not so many that they all deserved this sobriquet.

Yet last week, I was speaking to someone in the financial business, and he flatly said, "OK, I'm going to sign and fax back the contract."

It was a clear statement of intent. I thought the deal was tied up. But something about it didn't ring true.

Did he do what he promised? No, and I'm coming to feel that he explicitly lied.

But for what purpose? I hope it wasn't to be liked or to avoid disapproval.

Few things are higher on my don't-do list than to purposely mislead. I take some care in not leading people on, especially salespeople. Why waste everyone's time?

Nevertheless, here is an adage I first heard from Dun & Bradstreet, and I think all of us should keep it uppermost in our minds:

The deal isn't made until the money is paid.

You may have promises, and one party might have performed. But until cash passes hands, you have nothing. Perhaps you have a lawsuit, but that's no assurance of money either. It's worse. You'll invest good money chasing bad. Even if you are right, the judgment may go to the other party.

We need promises, execution of those promises, and money, to have a deal.

Even then, after the money has been paid, the payer might demand a refund. Deals can be undone too.

Buyers may or may not be liars. The key is to insist upon payment. You certainly have no deal without it.

Tip 31: The Games Managers Play

Sales managers and small-business owners always try to squeeze more from less. Typically, they don't want to invest more to get more. They want to pay less and get more.

That happens to be one definition of *productivity*. It's not one of my favorites, as you'll see. Management will say reining in sales costs is needed and completely justified, when really that's one major way they cost-justify their own jobs. They need to constantly retask you so they'll seem busy. If they're not selling, they don't produce much, except reports, and frequently demotivation.

Getting in your way *is* their job. Or at least they behave that way.

Here is a short list of the games sales managers play, which take direct aim at your wallet. They:

1. Use Tom Sawyer as their role model.
2. Move the goalposts.
3. Use team incentives.
4. Fire the secretaries and assistants.

5. Create distracting rivalries.

6. Make salespeople pay for overhead items.

7. Create chargeback systems, putting you in debt.

8. Reassign accounts frequently.

9. Split territories into smaller slices.

10. Make sellers quit, forfeiting their commissions.

Let's review these in more detail.

1. *Use Tom Sawyer as their role model.* Remember Tom Sawyer's genius? He got his pals to paint his auntie's fence for free, positioning labor as fun and as a perk, a privilege. Then he actually charged them a fee to work for free.

Sales managers will require you to attend a training session at headquarters in Muncie, Indiana, but they'll call it a working vacation. You'll have at least a half day on Saturday morning to enjoy the pleasures and treasures of nearby Indianapolis. (Of course, you're flying home on Saturday night, because fares are often cheaper.)

2. *Move the goalposts.* Managers are also fond of moving the goalposts, especially if you seem to be scoring sales too easily. Instead of having to sell twenty widgets to qualify for a bonus, suddenly you'll need to hit twenty-three. Hey, that's only asking you to be 15 percent more efficient, correct? You're not going to whine about that, are you?

3. *Use team incentives.* Managers are fond of saying there is no *I* in the word *team*. There are no dollar signs either.

Pooling commissions is a clever way to pay sellers less. Plus, it neatly makes sellers manage and motivate each other. Those that underachieve are fragged by their mates and pushed into early retirement because they aren't pulling their weight.

4. *Fire the secretaries and assistants* (I know: what's a secretary?), pushing their work onto you. This means you'll be tasked with inputting and editing countless files in your CRM system. The sales manager will moan, "Gee, I have to do all of *my* work on my own too!" Those are crocodile tears, because that's pretty much all they do anyway: clerical work.

5. *Create distracting rivalries.* Creating interteam rivalries makes salespeople fight each other instead of fighting management. Unfortunately, there are side effects. In every contest that someone wins, everyone else feels like a failure. They also come to think the game is rigged.

And it could be rigged. I worked at one company where I was ahead in a contest at the end of the closing day. Somehow, miraculously, the number-one sales guy came out on top when we reopened after the holiday break.

Contests distract us from focusing where it counts: on customers. Those rivals management has set us up to beat are not paying our way. They're getting in the way.

6. *Make salespeople pay for overhead items.* I worked in a company where I was promised a draw against com-

missions. Most people that bought from us used charge cards. My manager never told me that I would be charged a 3 percent fee on every sale paid for that way. Then I was slammed for the fee when I saw my first check. This is simply a cost of doing business that most firms absorb. It is overhead. But they'll try to pass along garbage charges like this to you. Beware!

There was an alternative. If you got people to pay by check or by an instant transfer of funds known as an ACH, you could avoid the fee. After learning about this alternative, I tried to push people into using the ACH, which wasted my time.

7. *Create chargeback systems, putting you in debt.* A number of companies force salespeople to pay into a reserve fund that will be used to defray costs when customers charge back, which means when they cancel or don't pay. This could be 10–15 percent of your accrued sales commissions. Say you earned $5000 in a given pay period. As much as $750 of that could be held back. That's a chunk! You'll be told that these funds will be released to you after clients pay in full or a certain amount of time elapses. That could be three to six months hence.

Management knows that a lot of folks will quit or be fired, leaving lots of dough in the chargeback fund. There is also the nasty possibility that you'll experience a number of cancellations through no fault of yours. But because of their timing, they could overwhelm your salary or be reduced from the amount you're being paid in your draw.

8. *Reassign accounts frequently.* Another game is reassigning accounts and leads to other salespeople. One company reassigned new leads after twenty-one days. If you didn't close an account, it went to someone else, who then held it for a similar period. A lead could have multiple handlers within four or five months. In many places, reassignment is done on an ad hoc basis. You never know when the rug will be pulled out from under you. But if you know you're going to lose a lead in two days, won't you be inclined to overwork it, to the detriment of other, potentially more rewarding prospects?

9. *Split territories into smaller slices.* Sales managers have probably been splitting sales territories for a hundred years. "We've determined there's far more potential in your region than we're tapping right now. That's why we're giving half of it to Ralph." This could mean your sales will take a 50 percent hit, and your commissions too. It could signify an even greater loss to you if your best accounts are being carved away and put on someone else's plate.

10. *Make sellers quit, forfeiting their commissions.* Every seasoned manager knows how to make people quit "voluntarily." They do this by curbing your opportunities, stalling in paying you, casting evil glances, and other methods. Suddenly they may start calling your prospects just to check up on you. They may ask you to reprogram your voice mail so if you're not picking up the line, the call will be handled by a "buddy," who will either split commissions with you or earn them all by herself.

What's your instinctive reaction to being on deck with a job that's sinking away from you? It is to jump off NOW.

Games sales managers play makes no sense. They seem nutty and counterproductive. When you experience them firsthand, as I have, they're outright brutal. What can you do to counteract them, to defend against demotivating sales managers? Avoid them as much as you can. I expand on this tip in the next section.

Tip 32: Work Remotely and Sell Better

Recently I took a working vacation in Italy. In Rome, by day, my family and I did the sights. We saw the Sistine Chapel and St. Peter's Basilica, went to various museums, and took some side trips, including one to a surprisingly snowy Florence.

By late afternoon, I started to work in earnest. I plugged in my laptop and headset. I made and returned calls back to the States, sent out brochures and information, closed deals, and moved others through the typical sales pipeline. I worked until midnight, more or less, and then repeated the drill.

While I had some technical issues with phoning, the experience was mostly positive. In fact, my takeaway from it is that you really can work from anywhere these days, especially if you do much of your selling over the phone and by email.

Why go into the office at all if you can avoid it?
There are some solid reasons for staying away.

Offices can be toxic, literally and figuratively. The ventilation can be spotty, and they're notoriously too cold or too hot. They're breeding grounds for the flu.

They can also be emotionally toxic. For example, at one site there was a sales bullpen. I sat next to a guy that whined his way through conversations. He complained about prospects, telling me in whimpering detail about the ones that got away.

The nasty sales manager who is always in your face *isn't*—if you aren't face-to-face. Sure, there's instant messaging, which keeps you tethered to these personalities, but it is a very thin and loose tie.

Above all, when you telecommute, you save commuting time. For me, this has ranged up to three and a half hours per day on the road. That translated into 130 miles a day, or 2860 a month, or 34,320 miles per year.

Remember, I was in the car leasing business. Believe me when I tell you that kind of high mileage is a car killer, and it incurs a huge expense in maintenance and depreciation.

In my case, it also took a toll on me. Forget about fatigue for a minute. What's really taxing is to have up to three and a half hours of lost productivity or even potential time to yourself or with loved ones leached away from you. This loss was deeper and more damaging when I used to commute by plane to sell and consult with clients.

The counterargument is when you're away, you miss a lot of fun interactions, important gossip, and actual opportunities to impress the honchos.

I say these don't enhance selling; they compete against it.

If you can work remotely, even for a day or two per week, do it. It could open a new world to you!

Tip 33: Keep Your Sales Secrets *Your* Secrets!

My dad used to set up his appointments by phone. He did it from home, which ties into my last point about working remotely if you can.

Primarily, he did not want others in the office to hear his techniques. He didn't want to be cloned or imitated. He didn't want to dilute his mystique. He also wanted to be left alone and free to say things the way he wanted to say them, without feeling he was in a fishbowl.

Your techniques are not nothing. They're important property interests. Look at them as if they are the secret formula to Coca-Cola, which is famously locked in a secure vault. Coke is not going to blab about its recipe. It is worth billions of dollars.

Don't go out of your way to reveal all you know to anyone. In fact, not doing that is known as the Scheherazade approach, used by highly paid speakers.

You'll recall that Scheherazade was a captured princess whose captor was going to kill her. She held him off by telling him stories night after night. Each installment was a cliff-hanger. That led to another day of living, and to an increasingly bewitched captor.

If you're a merchant, you cannot afford to give away the store, your stock in trade. Why would successful sellers want to give away their wealth?

There are answers to that. One reason is that they crave recognition for being clever. That is a secondary-gain trap, which I have discussed in another section.

You're the magician. Create awe and wonder. Never reveal the secrets behind the tricks. Once the word gets out, the trick will become useless.

Tip 34: Negotiate in Advance to Be Paid Your Commissions and Residuals upon Leaving

More than once I've mentioned that sales managers and companies act irrationally, or at any rate mainly in their self-interest.

Knowing this, you have to look out for yourself. Some wise person said you don't get what you deserve; you get what you can negotiate. You'll be ten times more effective negotiating before you're hired than once you're on board.

Most sellers fail to bargain for being given their unpaid commissions and residuals upon severing ties.

Here's the scenario: You quit your job for greener pastures. You have hundreds or thousands or even tens of thousands of dollars in unpaid commissions. Do you automatically forfeit them when you part company? Generally you do. You make a big sacrifice to leave.

Acknowledging this fact, you may be able to negotiate with the new firm to defray your losses by providing you with a signing bonus in one form or another. But this is not customary, and it takes effort.

I think it's far better to bargain with the company to be paid commissions and other residuals for a set period of time, say for six months to a year, after you leave. Make sure to boilerplate the agreement with the proviso that you will be paid whether you voluntarily or involuntarily empty your locker.

Look: when you quit or are fired, it costs you money. Your bills need to be paid during the transition from one shore to another.

Why should companies have an incentive to get you to fill your pipeline with commissionable deals and then be free to stiff you?

Tip 35: Never Lose Your Cool

The last chapter of my book *Dr. Gary S. Goodman's 77 Best Practices in Negotiation* details some of the big blunders I've made in bargaining. Many have come as a result of losing my cool. I took offense over something trivial.

For example, I had a meeting with a major opinion-research company whose name you're quite familiar with. We had reached the end of a meeting, and I was being walked to the door by a fellow who was part of the proceedings. He was a lawyer by training, and he seemed hostile toward me.

"We're going to need a noncompete agreement!" he barked.

And I shot back, "I'll need one too."

That blew the deal.

I should have bitten my tongue and grumbled to myself in the car. This would have given me time to cool off and consider a more reasoned approach.

In retrospect, a noncompete agreement would not have been unbearable. My reaction was really saying, "I don't need you."

Strictly speaking, this was true. I had a big enough bankroll to not do the deal. But it was stupid to lose my cool.

On another occasion, I was returning from a preliminary consulting engagement with a charge-card company in Arizona. That event went fairly well. I was invited to submit a proposal for a longer engagement.

On the plane home, I carelessly composed the proposal, and my cavalier attitude protruded. I overstated their need for my services by characterizing their current practices as not quite evolved.

You don't sell well by attacking or insulting your prospects.

Here are the six messages that researchers tell us will make customers and prospects feel defensive and will make them go out of their way to not buy from you:

1. *Evaluation*. People don't like to feel that they're bozos. If we seem judgmental about them personally, they'll take offense. Typically they'll respond in kind. That lawyer said, "We'll need a noncompete," and I echoed the exact thing.

2. *Control.* If you constantly interrupt people or otherwise seem to be forcing them against their will, they won't go along. People don't want to feel like helpless objects that can be moved around the chessboard.

3. *Strategy.* I was trying to sell someone, but I suspected she was going to flatly reject the deal if I answered her detailed questions by phone. Brusquely, I said, "All of this information will be in the documents I'm sending to you." My avoidance led her to reject my offer anyway.

4. *Neutrality.* When selling, you don't want to seem too eager to close the deal. You shouldn't press for a yes too hard or too often. On the other hand, you don't want to commit the opposite sin, which is acting callously indifferent: "I couldn't care if you say yes or no" or "I work on a salary, not commission, so if you buy or don't buy, it doesn't impact my paycheck." They'll think, "If you don't care, then neither do I!"

5. *Superiority.* Don't come across as superior to the buyer. Of course you know more than they do about your product or service, but they're the authority when it comes to whether they'll like you enough to buy from you. Don't offend them by boasting about your great house or car or anything else.

6. *Certainty.* Similarly, the know-it-all offends nearly everyone. I'm sure you've run into people that believe they are authorities on everything. Usually they are good

at one thing—if they're lucky. My uncle was like this. A Harvard-educated lawyer, he occupied an exalted status as a walking encyclopedia. At best, this put the rest of us into a love-hate relationship with him.

Happily, there are six complementary messages that reduce and prevent defensiveness. They are:

1. Description
2. A problem-and-solution orientation
3. Spontaneity
4. Empathy
5. Equality
6. Flexibility

As a memory aid for remembering these supportive messages, I've crafted this line:

"Gee, I'm sorry to hear you say that. Let's see where we can go from here."

Into that one sentence, I've packed all of the supportive messages.

"Gee" is spontaneity.

"I'm sorry" is empathy.

"You said that" describes what was uttered. It doesn't evaluate it. It is a problem-and-solution orientation.

"Let's" is equality. "Let us" says, "We're in this together."

"See where we can go from here" suggests there are options to be explored. I'm not controlling the outcome. We have flexibility. We have choices.

Not losing your cool is important. I keep mine when I resist the temptation to lash back at a personal jab or negative remark. Before I react, I tell myself, "Gee, what I just heard could produce a defensive reaction from me. I'll choose a supportive response instead."

Sometimes just remaining silent will let the zingers swoosh past your ears.

We can't control what buyers or our workmates say, but we can choose our responses.

Keeping your cool will pay off handsomely. You'll also feel great because you didn't rise to the bait.

Tip 36: Make a Ceremonial Display of Working Hard to Reinforce Your Value

The great artist Pablo Picasso was having lunch with a few people when he drew something supersimple but very attractive on a napkin.

"May I have that?" one of the guests asked.

"For $25,000 you can have it," Picasso responded with a sly smile.

"Twenty-five thousand! Why, that only took you a minute to do!" the flabbergasted admirer remarked.

"Yes, but it has taken me fifty years to learn how to do that," Picasso countered, putting the napkin into his pocket.

Picasso knew his value, you have to agree. But in another sense he made a mistake that you don't want to replicate. He allowed the people at the table to come backstage to watch him work and to falsely conclude how "easy" it was for him to draw his spectacular pieces.

If you're a genius, as he was, then what you touch almost instantly turns to gold. I've noticed this in many professionals, whether they're dentists, attorneys, or salespeople. As a general rule, the gifted ones work fast, and seemingly without great exertion.

However, our society imputes much value to people who seem to be working hard, breaking a sweat. Ironically, the people who are sweating the most are amateurs and beginners.

It pays to develop a ceremony for those that are watching or monitoring you. A ritual will invest your work with more value.

A tip: appear to be toiling assiduously, instead of zipping through things.

Realtors, for example, put together elaborate marketing plans to convince sellers to list their properties. Most of the proposal is boilerplate, used again and again for every prospective client. But it is one pretty artifact, nicely bound and presented. It sends this message: "A lot of work and money was put into this, so I have earned your business!" The proposal creates a sense of entitlement and a feeling of obligation in the prospect to reciprocate.

One of my clients scripted the following expression into its sales presentations. This captures the feeling:

"It may seem like nothing is happening to you during this time, but a lot is going on behind the scenes."

In other words, we're working hard and earning our fees.

After doing some math, I asked a very prominent public-relations pro how he could charge multiple client retainers when he had limited clock time to service them all.

"What do you say to people who might raise that as a concern?" I asked.

"I tell them I'm thinking about my clients and cases all the time," he responded with the tranquillity of a Zen monk.

Another person might reply, "I multitask," but it doesn't convey the same cache.

The point is, you need to appear to be earning your keep. The greater the profit margin you seem to have, the greater is the need to dramatize your toil.

Sometimes it's smarter to actually work harder. My point here is that it is always smart to *appear* to be working hard.

Tip 37: Never Sit on Your Money!

"Rob asked Bob several times if he could wait a day or two to cash his check," an employee of a firm confided to me.

Apparently Rob, the accounting firm's owner, was experiencing cash-flow issues.

Alarm bells went off inside of me as I heard this bit of scuttlebutt. It's never good when firms are having trouble meeting their payrolls. One of the chief reasons they go under is poor cash management. And this was an *accounting firm*, for gosh sakes! They knew better.

As a consultant, I was paid differently, but from the moment I heard about this state of affairs, I was glad that I had long before developed the habit of depositing my checks as fast as I could reach a bank or ATM.

As it turned out, the canary that sniffed gas in the accounting mine—the fellow that disclosed the cash-flow problem—was sitting on his checks, not cashing them in a timely way.

He got stuck when the company suddenly shuttered its doors.

Salespeople that become lazy about getting paid don't do themselves any favors. They want to make nice and play well with others. So instead of insisting on getting every penny owed to them in a timely manner, they let things slide and end up taking losses.

My first white-collar job, at eighteen, was at a finance company. I was a collector of consumer debts. I learned how important it is to be both firm and civilized in demanding that monies be paid immediately when due. That training has helped me throughout my career. I simply don't let my clients get into arrears. Whenever possible, I schedule progress payments that are deposited into my bank before I undertake a given chunk of work.

You cannot trust any employer that hires you until you have cashed that first check.

To assure they don't get too far behind, you should negotiate for shorter pay intervals. I prefer weekly pay. This keeps employers on good behavior. If they're going to stiff you, it will be for far less than if you're paid biweekly, twice per month, or monthly.

There is another serious advantage to this. You'd be surprised at the number of financial wizards that you'll work for that think $16,000 a month equals $4000 a week.

Let's say you're negotiating your salary and they offer $16,000 per month. Tell them your personal budget is set up to operate weekly, so you need to be paid $4000 per week. There are roughly 4.333 weeks in a month. Multiplied by $4000, that comes to $17,332 per month. You've killed two birds.

Weekly pay reduces your risks and it gives you an instant raise!

I was consulting in New York for a Wall Street financial firm. As is my custom with shorter engagements, I require a deposit of 50 percent of my fee to reserve the dates and then 50 percent on arrival at the site.

I arrived, but no check was waiting for me. I had to wait until the end of the week, when my consulting concluded, to receive it, I was told.

No problem, I thought. They have to be good for it.

At the end of my schedule, I tracked down the person that coordinated my sessions, and he gave me the check. Immediately I walked across the street to deposit it at a branch of the international bank that I use.

The teller said, "Excuse me, sir, but this check isn't signed."

"It isn't signed?" I echoed.

She was right.

I marched back into the building, and it took several minutes for me to find my contact. Instead of telling me

I'd have to go to accounting, he was senior enough to sign it himself, which he did with a perplexing grimace. Off I went to the bank, and the deposit went through.

To this day, I don't know what was really going on. Was it a mere oversight? Was it purposeful? Was I supposed to discover the error when I returned to California, thousands of miles away? And then would they try to strong-arm me into accepting less as the price of issuing a good check?

Those of us that are students of negotiation know that there is a dirty trick called "the mistake that isn't a mistake." For example, some people try to take advantage of you by accepting your package, but when they pay the invoice, they fail to include shipping and handling. Hoping you'll let it slide, or perhaps think you didn't mention that they'd have to pay for shipping, they force you to contact them and to confront the issue. A lot of people are conflict-averse, and they will let this "mistake" go.

What made me go immediately to the bank with the check in that pay envelope? It was that adage which has become a mantra with me, learned long ago.

Never sit on your money!

If you do, you'll be shooting yourself in the wallet.

Tip 38: Continually Improve Your Sales Skills

It's a no-brainer to say you should always improve your sales skills. But less than 10 percent of career sellers make this a priority.

First, what do I mean by *improving*?

Improvement means trying new techniques. They could be ages-old and hand-me-downs from sales authors, but they'll be new to you. If you haven't tried them, you won't know what they can achieve for you.

New techniques are everywhere if you're keen on spotting them. If you're selling in a bullpen, it's easy to detect them. Anything that is said that you haven't heard before can be a source. Plus, if there are top sellers that seem to use the same familiar scripts, clearly new angles are contained in them.

Borrow these phrases, because if they're in the air, it's only fair. They belong to everyone, right?

I was consulting for a firm that sold business opportunities. Clients were financed. They'd put down an initial payment of 20–50 percent, and the company would allow them to pay the rest of the fee over twelve months.

A lot of these buyers were new entrepreneurs who didn't have the self-discipline or enduring motivation to last twelve months. So they gave up, and this meant they become slow-pays or no-pays. Their accounts had to be sent to collections, and a large proportion became write-offs. Sellers were paid on collected dollars, so if clients stopped paying their monthlies, sellers lost money.

One fellow changed everything. He started getting new clients to pay in full, in record numbers. Typically, 10-20 percent paid their fees in full.

He got 80 percent to do it.

Smart sellers around him began to imitate him, and the company average quickly rose to about 65 percent.

This one technique revolutionized the business. For one thing, sellers made a lot more money, and they made it immediately. They didn't have to wait. The default rate plummeted, because fewer clients were stringing out their payments. So the company prospered.

The outside collection agency was fired. It was no longer needed. And the motivation of the sales team skyrocketed.

Everyone benefitted!

Your selling skills are really your major capital. They represent wealth, so it makes sense to add to them, just as you would try to put money into investments.

I urge you to push your employers to send you to sales seminars. Not only is this a refreshing break in routine, but you'll learn a ton.

You don't have to, of course. As many of my seminar attendees have said, "If I only get *one* technique out of this class I can use, this will have been time well invested."

The courses you take also become résumé fodder. They'll look good when you apply for your next position. You'll have a legitimate claim to being paid more than other applicants. And you'll stay fresh. This is crucial, because routines, however successful, can become boring.

Don't let bad habits break the monotony. Try novel techniques and watch what happens. You'll bring fresh enthusiasm to your delivery, and that will earn more sales for you.

Plato said that knowledge is the only good thing we cannot get too much of. Ice cream will make you fat if you binge on it, but new techniques will fatten your wallet.

Binge on them!

Tip 39: If You Don't Make Them Feel, You Won't Get the Deal

I was just talking to a prospect a few minutes ago. I asked him a little about his business and his goals.

"I want to expand," he said.

Then he went on to tell me how his body shop needs to raise some money fast to rebuild its painting booths. Because new cars are starting to use aluminum construction, an entirely new environment needs to be created to paint the vehicles capably and safely. Insurance companies won't refer business to him if he doesn't upgrade his facilities.

While I was listening, he interrupted himself. "You seem like a nice guy," he said. Then he started asking questions about my offer. He warmed up. He could visualize becoming one of my clients.

The key is that he *felt something*. He liked me. All things being equal, people will choose to buy from people they like. If they don't feel a connection to you, they'll sit and wait, or they'll simply say no, or offer a spurious objection.

Some of us forget this fact or are even hostile towards it. We believe people should buy based on logic alone. If something pencils out, then it's obvious! Buy it! Or if we believe so strongly in the desirability of our widget that we think people should be immediately wooed by our assessment.

They may be, but it will probably require they like you first.

Or you may be able to make a different emotional connection. We know that there are sourpusses in the buying community. They're grumpy and obstreperous, and nothing will please them or make them like anything or anyone.

Then find something they hate that you hate and agree with them. They hate the weather they've been having. So do you.

Sometimes we need to make them dream. This means opening them up to talk about their goals and aspirations. Let them wax on about all that they hope to accomplish. Better yet, ask them how they're going to put your product or service to work. This path takes them on a trip of the imagination, and they'll buy that picture, because it's theirs.

Making them fearful is very risky. I've seen a lot of research that says high fear messages fail, because people block them out.

"If you smoke, you'll die!" is one type of appeal that was tested, and people almost universally countered that it wouldn't happen to them.

But when a low fear message was used, it was more persuasive. "If you smoke, you won't smell good, you'll cough a lot, and your teeth will get stained" was the type of message that got more people to quit or cut back their consumption.

Building a better mousetrap won't make people beat a path to your door. You have to get them to feel an urgent need to solve their pest problem.

You may not be a feeling type and even believe it should be unnecessary to evoke sentiment in others.

Perhaps, but it works nonetheless.

Tip 40: Style-Shift:
Sell in and out of Your Comfort Zone

Some of the world's greatest philosophers have concluded that a major source of human misery comes from resisting what is.

It's foggy outside, and you hate fog. You start ranting about the weather, which you can't control, apart from going indoors. You transform an unpleasant state of affairs into an "awful" one.

Same thing happens when we rant about certain kinds of prospects. Fence-sitters are my favorites to disparage. They can't make up their minds. We spend inordinate amounts of time and energy on them.

"Why can't they be like most and simply say yes or no?" we wonder.

The fact is that there are 50–80 percent of prospects that you won't be able to close. That is, you won't close them with your current selling style. This isn't awful, providing that the 20 percent or more that you are capable of closing supply you with enough compensation for your efforts.

Even if that's true, wouldn't it be nice to garner at least a few more customers?

The way that's going to happen is by style-shifting.

Let's go back to those fence-sitters that I find so frustrating. My favorite buyers make fast decisions; we know this. And my presentations are designed to elicit quick approvals.

What can I do with the fence-sitters? Two things come to mind.

I can ease off the throttle, calm down, and give them lots of room to ruminate. See them as cattle that even under the best of conditions aren't going to be transformed into racehorses.

I'm reminded of Jane Goodall's research on chimpanzees. She very gradually ingratiated herself. At first, she sat down in a remote location and gave the group a chance to smell her from afar and to acclimate to her presence. Then, gradually, she repositioned herself closer and closer. Finally, she got to a point where they accepted her as just a funny-looking chimpanzee.

Yup, becoming one of them—that's the price you pay sometimes to get a fence-sitter to budge and to buy.

The second approach is to become even more directive, to make the buying decision for them. For this purpose, I like to use two closes. The assumptive checkback close sounds like this:

"So let's start on the eleventh, and I'm sure you'll be pleased, OK?"

I'm making the decision, am I not? I suggested we start, I selected the date, I assured the prospect all would go well, and crucially, I tied it down with an "OK?"

Imagine the prospect counters with, "The eleventh won't work."

"OK, then we'll make it the twelfth."

That is the power-assumptive close. I don't check it back with an OK. I make the decision all by myself.

What's a fence-sitter to do?

Surely (I know: don't call you "Shirley"), there will be some that will resist. "I still need to think it over," they might offer.

"Well, I appreciate that, but we need to reserve the date now. Otherwise you'll be faced with paying double or missing out entirely, and you don't want that, do you?"

Here I'm closing based on urgency and scarcity. These lures are used all the time.

Watch one of those shopping channels or go online and you'll see, "Only one left at this price!" For many, the fear of losing is a more potent persuader than the prospect of gain.

My point here is not to catalogue the various ways of getting fence-sitters to buy. I'm using this as an example to show we need to style-shift to start closing those that have been resisting our conventional persuasive approaches.

Let me give you a dramatic example of style-shifting and working outside of your comfort zone.

In my twenties, I was a successful salesperson and then a sales manager and trainer. I made good money.

I earned my way through college and graduate schools. With my PhD in hand, after five years of university teaching experience, I struck out on my own as a consultant.

I was pretty hot stuff in the classroom. Not an easy grader, I was well liked and highly rated. Then I became part of a training cohort hired by the U.S. Navy. Our task was to train 18,000 senior-level managers in eighteen months. It was a mammoth endeavor, the largest Navy civilian-management training program in history.

Part of our prep was being observed and videotaped teaching a group in Cape Cod, Massachusetts. Frame by frame, my instructors dissected my style. The first thing they said was, "Who is that guy?" pointing to me on the screen.

"That's me, of course."

"That couldn't be you, because you're not smiling. Why do you look so serious, so grave?"

I was wearing my college-professor face, not my adult educator–Navy trainer face. I was out of character, they said.

At first I felt a little defensive. I was a hit as a speaker, I was highly rated, and my students learned, darn it!

But I thought about the critique overnight, along with their simple suggestion.

"Smile more!" they urged. So I did. At first it was hard. I had been very ego-involved in my college-professor persona. But the results were astonishing. With the other training tips I learned, my evaluations nearly reached a level of perfection.

After the Navy program concluded, I estimate that my training from them enabled me to earn at least a million dollars on top of what I would have brought in with only my former skills. I sold and delivered bigger and bigger programs.

I could point out for you how a good seminar is constructed like a good sale, but that would be overstepping the topic at hand.

My point is that you should be prepared to operate out of your comfort zone, to stretch, to style-shift.

It could be worth a fortune to you as well!

Tip 41: Remember Your Aristotle

Aristotle was a practical philosopher whose treatise on persuasion, *The Rhetoric*, is still highly valued and studied worldwide.

This book presents a powerful device: a three-part model for persuasion that adapts nicely to selling. Aristotle says there are three sources of persuasion to which speaker should look: *ethos, pathos,* and *logos.* If you use all three in your selling, you'll be bound to earn sales from more people, because you'll be appealing to three significant types of buyers.

Yesterday I was on the phone with a prospect who responded to an Internet ad. After I asked him some questions and told him I'd email details, he said:

"Will I see your website and credentials in what you're sending me?"

I assured him he would indeed, along with an A+ rating from the Better Business Bureau.

For this buyer, ethos is the most important characteristic in a vendor. *Ethos* refers to the character of a person or a company. How credible are you, and what sources of ethical proof can you marshal in your selling? These would be indications of trustworthiness such as ratings, awards, prominent achievements, and professional affiliations.

A licensed general contractor has more credibility, and higher ethos, than an unlicensed handyperson. Licensing brings with it the burden of professional scrutiny, certification, and regular recertification, but the benefit is that it is a persuasive shortcut to say, "We've been licensed and in good standing for twenty-five years." That creates instant trust, and for some prospects trustworthiness is the key that unlocks the desire to buy.

Joe Girard, reputedly the world's greatest car seller, found gold in using a certain type of ethos. He built bridges of identification so buyers would think, "He's a lot like me."

Perceived similarity is a very significant source of ethos. Girard would ask, "Where do your kids go to school?"

"Great, my kids went there!" he'd beam.

"Is Mrs. Stumpus still the first-grade teacher?"

"I had the dealership donate to that campus cleanup drive a few years back."

With a few exceptions, we prefer to buy from people we can relate to, who seem similar to us. Sellers tell jokes not only to put customers in a good mood, but to show that their sense of humor is the same as the prospect's.

The exception to the perceived-similarity precept is in the area of expertise. We don't want our surgeons and attorneys to be regular folks like us when they perform their professional duties. In that regard, we're happier when their competence is entirely different, and the more expert they are, the better.

Pathos is the second source of persuasion in the Aristotelean model. *Pathos* refers to the emotions. When you make this sort of appeal, it is called *emotional proof.*

Sellers often tell stories about people that chose not to purchase, with disastrous results. Insurance agents are known to talk about the perils of underinsuring, buying less coverage than one needs. Then, when a claim is made, the insured is shocked to find their policy doesn't restore them to their prior condition, economically or otherwise.

Pathos isn't always negative—far from it. Seeing smiling Girl Scouts with their moms stationed outside of your supermarket summons a whole set of positive emotions. For one, it is the image of wholesomeness. Scouting is a great character-building activity, and being associated with it, even through buying a few boxes of cookies, feels good.

Anytime the tagline "You'll be happy you did!" or "You won't regret it!" appears, you know pathos is being appealed to.

"Act quickly—there are only three left at this price!" is an emotional appeal that taps into two very potent buying stimuli: urgency and scarcity. As I've already noted, many experienced sellers believe that without urgency and scarcity, people won't have enough motivation to act.

I consulted to a company that uses these tools quite frequently. They'll say that they have a container coming in from China with a 100 gross of a certain widget, so buy your ten or twenty gross today.

The next week, they'll fax a note that says, "Only sixty gross are left! Reserve yours now!"

The following week, they'll be down to twenty-five gross.

Then, just before the ship docks at the harbor, they'll fax a note that says, "Sorry, none left. All sold out. Thank you!"

They'll wait a few weeks and repeat the same countdown clock on a different item that's being imported.

This works unbelievably well. People want a bargain. They compete with each other if an auction atmosphere is created. (Just look at the huge success of eBay.) And they don't want to lose out. Pathos is a powerful motivation.

Aristotle's third source of persuasion is *logos*, reason. When you use logical proof, you are appealing to people's rational faculties, providing good reasons for them to buy.

"Buy this solar-panel system, and it will pay for itself immediately in utilities savings."

Many buyers, particularly in business, insist that pro-
posals pencil out, that they be cost-justified.

I was able to market cost-intensive customer service training programs involving six- and seven-figure
investments. I did not sell them because my prospects
wanted to please their customers, but because I was able
to demonstrate precisely how the projects would reduce
their costs. The fact that their people would be better
service providers came along with the savings as an extra
perk that they received for free.

Use ethos, pathos, and logos in your sales presentations and collateral sales materials. Establish your credibility, arouse the right emotions, and appeal to logic and
to common sense, because these are the three reasons
most people buy.

Tip 42: Should You Succeed Immediately in a Sales Position?

I had this theory about winning at blackjack. In a single-
deck situation, with few or no other players at the table,
the dealer could only beat me so many times in a row.
That number might be three or four or five, and then my
turn to win would come around.

I'd bet accordingly. I'd bet the minimum and lose.
Put up the same, and lose. Do it a third time, and that's
right—I'd lose the third hand.

Then I'd bet big.

Let's say I lost that one—gosh, that would hurt! But
if it was the same deck he was dealing from, I'd double

the previous bet, which meant I went absolutely, utterly, irretrievably huge. And I won. Call for a new shuffle, and repeat the cycle.

There wasn't any science to this, but it was a system. The key to doing it well was simply applying patience.

I came under a little scrutiny in casinos, because they thought I was card-counting, when really I was hand-counting, which is very different.

I give you this example to point out that as a salesperson you can only lose so many deals until you start winning. This is important to know. Plus, sometimes you win right away, and sometimes you don't.

When rejection begins, most of us do the opposite of what I did at blackjack.

We go huge with our first bets, giving every deal over-the-top enthusiasm. Let's say we're rebuffed, for whatever reason. Then we cut back emotionally. We distance ourselves, guarding our egos from the next rejection.

We lose the next deal. Same pattern occurs. More distancing is done, and we actually anticipate rejection.

We might put pebbles into our own shoes, disabling ourselves by nervously overtalking. Or we might invite rejections by trying to anticipate all possible objections and then by inserting them prematurely into the conversation.

What happens in my blackjack system? You stay in the game long enough to start winning, and you ratchet up your enthusiasm with each no you hear. You realize that the payoff is just inches away, and you refuse to stop short of the finishing line.

What happens if you simply keep losing? You never get blackjack, and the dealer keeps busting you out?

That happened to me in blackjack, and I surrendered a lot of money.

It also occurred on one sales job. No matter how hard I tried, how clever I got, I simply couldn't buy a sale.

That's when you get philosophical. You tell yourself, "It wasn't meant to happen." And you move on. You might get lucky somewhere else.

That has happened to me quite a bit. For example, when I was in graduate school, I sold office supplies to augment my teaching income. I had heard over the years that there was good money to be made in that business, but it seemed from afar to be too high-pressure for my tastes. But realizing that I didn't want to live like a pauper while earning my doctorate, I answered an ad at the school's employment board.

"Hey, if they're advertising at USC's placement center, how bad can they be?" I thought.

I interviewed, and told them I had been the top gun at Time-Life and was ready to give this a shot.

"Right now? Do you want to get on the phone now and show us what you've got?"

"Sure, why not."

They had me listen to a guy that was selling pens to bakeries. I heard a call or two and the manager asked if I was ready.

He said, "Get a directory from that shelf, pick a number, and call it."

And I did, following the pitch to the letter. Bingo, I made one call and I made one sale. That put some nice change into my pocket.

As it turned out, my beginner's luck (or skill, if you prefer) portended great things. I made great money at that place part-time. It didn't interfere with my studies and teaching. In fact, it was a pleasant diversion from academia. It anchored me to the real world, and I looked forward to making calls, and of course money.

This "first try, first sale" phenomenon has repeated itself several times in my career.

I succeeded in my first attempt to get a university to sponsor my seminars. That conquest set the stage for distributing my programs through forty universities across the U.S. in short order. And those sponsors led directly to a number of other great opportunities. I've noticed over time that the cohort of sellers I have trained that succeed immediately is actually quite large.

So I suppose there are two ways to beat the odds. Let the house beat you a few times, as you grow your enthusiasm and increase your emotional investment. Or assign great significance to those sales situations in which you succeed right away, feeling like a natural.

Early success is great. It reassures those that hired you, and it reassures you that you made a good choice of a suitable sales situation. You can all relax and enjoy the nice start that you've made. That helps you to focus on the clients rather than becoming obsessed with yourself or with what veterans are thinking of you.

In any case, observe the pattern of your achieve-ments. It can tell you a lot.

Tip 43: Bad Courtships Signal Worse Marriages to Come

Nearly every sales room I've seen has inspirational quotes hanging. I'm fond of the one from legendary Green Bay Packers coach Vince Lombardi. Reduced to its essence, it says winning isn't a sometime thing, it is an all-the-time thing—a habit.

Winners never settle for second place or second-level bowl games, where losers play losers. The measure of a person is that he leaves everything on the playing field. He is never happy to leave the stadium a loser.

The other quote is from President Calvin Coolidge: "Persistence is supreme." None of the other virtues even come close. Talent is not so hot. There are talented dere-licts that never achieve any lasting things.

I'd like to focus on the second quote for now—the one about never giving up. Too little persistence is cer-tainly a vice. Sellers need to work their leads, and go the extra mile. But you don't want to go the extra twenty miles, and you certainly don't have the time or energy to be that exhaustive. Especially with new prospects, there are practical limits to the energy you should expend. You can multiply this sentiment for new prospects that are a hassle to deal with. You can be the greatest speaker in the world, but if your audience isn't listening, it doesn't matter.

It always takes two to make a sale. You can't do their buying for them. You can only do your part. When prospects frustrate your performance, putting huge boulders in your path, you can't interpret this as normal.

What do I mean? For example, they never make themselves available to have a decent, in-depth conversation. In most transactions involving professional sellers and not clerks, you have important things you need to go over. Prospects that truncate your routine, insisting you cut to the chase or pour your proposal into a thimble, are telling you they are probably not worth chasing. Nor is it a good sign if they tell you that you have to run a huge gauntlet before getting before the right set of eyes and ears.

Sure—if you are selling nuclear reactors to other countries, there's going to be a protocol. It may take ten years from the inception of your contacts to final construction of the facilities. But selling a new car shouldn't take months, because it won't be new anymore!

Early in my life I heard the following expression about romance: troubled courtships signal worse marriages to come. Getting together shouldn't be like Shakespeare's *The Taming of the Shrew* or Broadway's *Kiss Me, Kate*. A good pairing is more like *Kismet*. It seems fated to happen and to endure.

When prospects give you a rough time, chances are very good they're not going to be good partners going forward. Let's say they're price shoppers, and they posture that any vendor will do as long as the price is right. That's a disloyal customer talking, who will flee the instant he hears the siren song of a competitor's discount.

Persisting too much with these folks is more than foolhardy. It is yet another way to shoot yourself in the wallet. Not only is it wasteful and raucous bringing them aboard, but they make terrible "mates," who are seldom happy. They end up becoming customer-service nightmares, and in this era of the Internet, you'll pay dearly to keep them happy. Otherwise, they'll threaten to beef about you to the universe.

I realize you're in a delicate position as a salesperson. You can't give up on too many prospects before you're thought to be too high-strung. Yet you need to appreciate that you're selling your labor, which expresses itself in time allotted to various clients and prospects. Time is money to you. Spend too much, and you're wasting it.

Here's something to chew on. The most profitable deals in my experience are those that came together quickly. The ones that I had to struggle for, which took forever to close, ended up becoming overall minuses—net losses for me.

Sound familiar?

I wish I could offer a hard-and-fast rule: "After one month of courtship, sever ties and move on." But I can't. You'll need to apply good sense and discernment.

It will be worth it, though.

Tip 44: Don't Let Prospects Hypnotize You into Discounting

I was having a meeting with an executive at the Playboy Channel. There we were, in an arty, modern building on the famous Sunset Strip (an appropriate address, if you think about it).

Playboy may have sent someone to my public seminar, or they could have read one of my books. Somehow they discovered me and wanted to learn more about my sales and customer-service training.

Having been on TV and in studios several times, I had no illusions that I would bump into half-nude goddesses on my way to a conference room. But at the same time, one can hope.

I suppose a zillion things went through my mind before that meeting began. Could I really put the Playboy Channel on my promotional materials after finishing a successful program with them? What if I fell in love with the program and never wanted to leave? I was used to dealing with Fortune 500 companies, which aren't all that sexy or glamorous.

The stakes were certainly different. I was keenly interested in how they were going to negotiate with me. Glamorous clients try to hypnotize you. One of their goals is to get you to discount your fees and to cut your profit margins.

In this sense they're similar to others, but the main ploy of a glamour company is to convey the idea that "you're lucky to be in our presence!"

We help them along by telling ourselves they're right. After all, they're going to permit us a rare glimpse backstage. Like magicians that dupe mere mortals by the millions, they are going to pull back the curtain and make us insiders.

Thinking these thoughts is proof of their hypnotic potential. Suddenly a deal isn't about business; it's about much, much more, we whisper internally. Excitement, drama, thrills, and even bragging rights are implicated, you tell yourself. You can't buy this sort of experience. Feel fortunate they aren't charging you!

Against this backdrop, imagine the surge that went through me when that not unattractive executive asked me in a smoky, seductive voice: "Are you *excited* about working for the Playboy Channel?"

I was on the horns of a dilemma. If I replied in the affirmative, I'd be succumbing to the siren song of glamorous outfits. I'd be admitting that the hypnosis worked. That would set me up for discounting, which I was ardently against doing.

If I said no, then I would seem to be lying. What right-thinking teenager in my peer group didn't wonder what it would be like to work at Playboy? Now that I was a grown-up teenager, had anything really changed?

I hated her question. It was too clever, and as a salesperson and business owner it made me feel, uncharacteristically, speechless. I did mutter something, which didn't come out as clearly or as convincingly as I could have hoped.

Truthfully, I was jaded. This *was* going to be just another deal to me, and I had plenty at that point. My plate was full, not with exotic treats, but with the meat and potatoes of a good business.

The hypnotism that I'm speaking about occurs with any clients that seem to be offering perks. If the companies are in the news and have a high profile, you can be swayed into cutting them special deals as the cost of affiliating with them.

If they offer trade arrangements, tickets from airlines, and comps at hotels in Vegas or London, then they have something tangible they're tendering. In those cases, they should be taken seriously, because you're exchanging value for value.

Be especially wary of people who manipulate you by saying, "If this first deal goes well, then we have dozens of additional deals we can give you." Dazzling you with a future gold mine is a great way to get you to discount those few nuggets you're holding in your hand. Remember, there's no such thing as taking a loss on deal one and then making it up in volume. You'll only multiply your losses.

I suppose this idea was at the base of my ambivalence over working with the Playboy Channel. It might lead me to more show-business deals, which I didn't want. That would unbalance my portfolio and put me in a niche I didn't want to get stuck in.

Tip 45: A Split Commission Beats No Commission

In most companies where I've sold and consulted, I closed my own deals. Accounts were assigned, and it would have signaled weakness to peers and managers to admit I was having trouble bringing a deal across the finishing line. But this isn't an ideal setup, for one simple reason: a single selling style isn't a match for every prospect.

For example, when I was selling business opportunities, I would be assigned a certain type of prospect who simply rubbed me the wrong way. This was the cynical know-it-all, a person who knew the price of everything but the value of nothing. Worse, he wouldn't listen for more than one sentence before interrupting me, which is a giant pet peeve of mine. I'm an educator, and there are few things more frustrating than not being allowed to fully make a point.

I got one of these people on the line, but instead of duking it out with him, I asked politely, "May I put you on hold for a quick second?" Then I got the attention of a pal who was the most patient salesman I had ever met. "Mikey could tame this guy," I thought. I transferred him over, and they got along well. Sure enough, Mike closed the deal.

In itself, that is a great achievement. The company didn't lose; it won. It earned a sale and a profit. If I couldn't turn over the deal to someone like Mike, it would have gone to waste. Worse, our loss could have been a competitor's gain, compounding the error if the prospect bought from the enemy.

What made this T-O, or turnover, so smooth and easygoing was the fact that the sales team was allowed and even encouraged to split commissions. In the example I gave, Mike and I split the deal 50-50.

That's smart business. Dumb businesses discourage T-Os and commission splitting. They have this idea that sellers must stand on their own two feet, and if they can't close every type of person, they're fatally flawed and should be shown the door.

I believe, as one of Clint Eastwood's characters said in a movie, "A man must know his limitations."

If you spot someone that you're not going to mesh with, by all means substitute another salesperson from your team.

This doesn't mean you can't fix some flaws and improve. Perhaps I can work on my patience and start to close more of these know-it-alls. It's worth a try. But splitting a commission surely beats earning no commission at all.

If your company permits it, don't let your ego get in the way by insisting you *should* persuade everyone. That's an unrealistic expectation. If your company discourages asking for help when a deal gets stuck or seems out of reach for you, give some thought to changing companies. Because then they're being unrealistic, and they're shooting everyone in the wallet, including themselves.

Tip 46: Should You Take That Vacation?

Robert was doing pretty well, closing a good number of deals. Finally, he felt he was making progress in cracking his monthly nut. He even had a few dollars left over and had paid down his credit-card debts.

"It's now or never," he thought as he pondered doing what his wife had been pining for.

It had been seven long years since their last major vacation, and she wanted more than anything to go to Europe.

Robert found an ideal package. In six days and six nights, they'd see Paris and London. The trip would span eight days, but he'd only miss five days of office presence. He hadn't missed a workday and was known to be a stalwart and steady producer. So he informed his manager where he was going.

He even promised to telecommute from Europe. With Skype and his office's cloud CRM program, it was no sweat to see the sights by day and then get his work done starting in the late afternoon. In fact, it was very cool to be able to steal second base while keeping your foot on first. To be able to vacation and to work seamlessly felt like a dream.

Refreshed and upbeat, he returned to the office on the appointed Monday morning, with an astonishing amount of energy and very little jet lag. He was called into a meeting with his manager.

"How was Europe, Robert? Great, glad to hear it. There are a few changes we'll be making," the boss said with a sardonic smile.

Effective immediately, Robert's territory and compensation plans were both being curtailed. No specific reason was given, except that senior management felt productivity would be increased this way. It was a take-it-or-leave-it arrangement. For the time being, Robert took it, feeling the rug had been pulled out from under him.

"Was I being punished for taking a vacation?" he wondered. "Did they think I was making too much money? This was the first trip my family has taken in seven years!"

He didn't know what to think. Maybe it was simple jealousy. He went somewhere nice, and they didn't. Or they figured he wasn't suffering enough. The comp plan was too rich. Management was leaving too much dough on the table. It's time to make old Robert hungry again. And we'll set an example for everyone else!

Am I saying that you can never take a vacation? That if you dare to enjoy a perk, even for a week, your employer or the universe will punish you and imperil your livelihood?

That is pretty much what I'm saying!

You don't want to become an object of envy to your customers, internal or external. I've seen what envy in the workplace can do.

"She doesn't have to work, you know. Her husband cleans up as an executive for a pharmaceutical company." That damaging piece of gossip prevented an otherwise very capable individual from earning the raises and promotions she deserved.

So if you don't want to become an object of envy, do you want to be pitied?

To an extent, you do.

Like that Electrolux vacuum seller who donned frumpy attire and demonstrated machines that he shuttled about in a beat-up station wagon, instead of in his Cadillac, you need to allow customers and coworkers to feel superior.

Here are some of the notions your words and conduct need to convey:

You aren't working as a hobby. You need the money. You're supporting a lot of people (or good causes).

You're a lifer, committed to that job forever and a day.

You appreciate everything and every opportunity.

You never complain!

Back to that vacation—should you take one?

Yes, but why say you're going to Europe? Why not say you're thinking of driving to a state or national park? You're going someplace cheap, a place from which your associates won't ask for a trinket.

Isn't this pretending? Isn't it a lie? Frankly, it's none of their business where you're going and how you're living outside of the workplace.

If you are a trust-fund baby and you work for sheer pleasure, or to stay active, or for whatever reasons, they should be beyond the reach of your employers and your peers. There should be a division between who you are and what you do. There should be a front stage and a backstage. It is up to you to decide when and for whom to lift the curtain, if you decide to lift it at all.

Concealment is a part of your job as a seller. You don't want to overtalk about the disadvantages of your product, do you? Likewise, don't willingly introduce information that is incongruous with the role you're playing at work.

If you're a grunt, seem like a grunt. If you're a rock star, seem like that. But try not to seem like a rock star when you're surrounded by grunts.

Instead of applauding you, they'll throw rocks at you.

Tip 47: Just Say No to Capped Commissions

H. Ross Perot became one of the richest people in America, ran for the office of president of the United States, and built a number of corporate powerhouses. But he started his career at IBM, where it might have finished. He could have retired there if that company hadn't made a huge error. That error is being repeated in companies across the world.

Perot, like other IBM salespeople, had an annual quota to reach in order to justify his salary. In his final year at that company, Perot reached his quota by the end of January.

That is when things became career-altering. Perot's income was capped at quota, so this meant he had absolutely zero financial incentive to don the IBM suit and carry the IBM briefcase after January 31.

He complained, pointing to the absurdity of deleting the incentives for the best salespeople they had on board. IBM wouldn't budge, and Perot left. He started a computer-services company that became a giant. And you can be sure he never made the same error of capping his salespeople's commissions.

Why is it a mistake? For one thing, it tells a top seller, "You're making too much money!" and "You're too good at what you do!" These are ridiculous notions. Can a ballplayer be too good—or a brain surgeon, or a teacher?

It is also a prescription for hiring mediocre people, those that will be satisfied with artificially depressed earnings. But above all, it is dumb, because there are lots of other ways companies have of cutting the income of their top sellers.

I've mentioned a few already. Companies split territories. They take away salaries, putting everyone on straight commission. They remove or reduce car allowances, and other perks. But putting up a huge billboard that says, "We'll never allow our sellers to make big incomes" is just too dumb to justify.

My dad, as I mentioned, was a top salesperson. One year he was told his income would be capped. He asked why, and he got this answer: "We're capping it because you're making an embarrassing amount of money!"

"Who is embarrassed?" he asked.

"Well, you're making a lot more than your sales manager!"

"Yes, but if he wants that kind of money, he should return to selling!" Dad retorted.

Of course he didn't win the argument, and not long after, he separated from that company.

You might be thinking that caps are set so high in some cases that worrying about reaching them is misplaced. Perhaps, but it is the kind of absurdity that gnaws at you. And usually where there is one major absurdity, there are others.

If a place says they cap commissions, work somewhere else.

One more thing: There are some companies that put the phrase "uncapped commissions" in their employment ads. They think they're going to reel in the world's best sellers this way. But they don't deserve such high-class talent because there isn't much money to be made working for them.

Do the math of success, which I have explained in another section. If the entire comp package doesn't add up, you won't want to work at a place, whether or not the earnings are capped.

Tip 48: "Do You Smell That?" If You Don't, Move On!

There is an unforgettable scene in *The Color of Money*, a great movie with Paul Newman and Tom Cruise. Fast Eddie Felson (Newman) has taken the young Vincent Lauria (Cruise), a rising star among pool hustlers, under his wing. They walk into a pool hall with Cruise's girlfriend, Carmen (played by Mary Elizabeth Mastrantonio), and this brief but telling exchange takes place:

Fast Eddie says, "Do you smell that?"

Vincent Lauria says, "What, smoke?"

"No," says Carmen. Money."

Sales operations that are thriving have a sweet smell of money too. When you walk into them, it isn't always an olfactory signal you perceive. Maybe your eyes tell you something. You see there is a sales board in the room, and there are some really big earnings numbers on it. That can smell like money. Or on your way to the interview, you had to find parking spot in the company lot. Space after space was occupied by staffers' BMWs, Mercedes-Benzes, and Porsches.

Then you spotted it: a Ferrari, parked in front of the sign "Salesperson of the Month," right near the front door.

The best clues aren't detected by smell or sight but by sound. It is when people that work in sales come up to you, whisper, "There's a *lot* of money to be made here," and grin.

This has happened to me more than once, and each time it turned out to be true. I cleaned up.

But the opposite can be the case as well. You can step into poverty. I'll tell you what poverty smells like. People are agitated. They frown. They look you up and down with suspicion. You're feeling the negativity of a swirling snake pit. There isn't enough wealth to go around. Sellers think their slim pickings are going to get even slimmer with your arrival at the scene.

If you're desperate and a job is offered, you might make the error of accepting it. But when you feel everyone is being pinched, be assured that it's going to happen to you as well.

Selling requires a certain expansiveness of the spirit. We need to feel uninhibited, exuberant, hopeful, and professional. Impoverished settings send us the opposite signals. They make us feel inhibited, somehow smaller than we were when we walked through the door. That's no mood in which to make sales magic!

It isn't necessarily a gilded atmosphere that smells of money, at least the kind of money that will find its way into your pay envelope. I've worked in opulent settings where you couldn't make a dime. I've toiled in ugly quarters, tiny windowless rooms no larger than a closet, but I went home to the Four Seasons Hotel, where I rented an apartment by the month. But one way or another, you need to smell the money, or sense its presence. If you do not, then move on!

Tip 49: When the Going Gets Tough, the Tough Kick Back

My dad became a legend at the Wayne Pump Company, where he worked as a sales engineer. He was the top dog, so he was asked to give a speech at the annual sales banquet.

"Do you see the clock on the wall?" he started. "It doesn't mean anything. If you want to be a sales champion, you'll learn to ignore it, as I have done."

At that point, management thought Dad was going to extol the virtues of working 24/7 and putting in a 200 percent effort. But Dad went the other way and came to live in infamy for it.

"I sell when I want to, not when the clock tells me to!" he roared to a suddenly stunned group. "I wake up in the morning when my body feels like it. I don't use alarm clocks. I have a big breakfast in the field, and I may visit one prospect before noon. Maybe I'll see another one in the afternoon. But if I don't feel like selling, I know I'm not going to succeed. So I don't bother. And that's how I made it to the top!"

That is a pretty extreme viewpoint, wouldn't you say?

I think I abide a little more by the work ethic, and I've even been known to say it isn't a question of whether to work smart or to work hard; it's smarter to work harder. You can get too lazy and become careless. Sloth will catch up with you!

Still, what my dad said about not feeling well and selling is probably valid. How can you succeed when you're not in top form?

I can. For instance, I actually did an entire seminar in Massachusetts with laryngitis. I was on tour and caught a cold. The next thing I knew, I was barely able to whisper.

I had self-sponsored the seminar, dropping thousands on its promotion. I had a large contingent from an area phone company in attendance. I didn't want to let people down or forfeit a lot of money. So the show went on! They were a gracious and tolerant group, and I earned remarkably good evaluations, considering.

I've also sold when sick, plenty of times. While I wasn't 100 percent, I wasn't 0 percent either.

But most folks I know can't do this. You may know that you aren't worth a darn when you're under the weather. Don't fight your nature. Take a nap if you need to. Cut back on your schedule.

My dad underscored his little talk with these words, "The early bird gets the worm. But that's *all* he gets—worms!"

Extreme? Without a doubt, but Dad knew himself, and he thrived.

Tip 50: Hook Up with Companies That Offer Great Perks

Some of the happiest salespeople I've known have worked for airlines. They earned decent money, but the perks made the job worth far more than the money.

They got flying privileges for themselves and for their immediate family members. They also got 50 percent and more off on the best hotels around the globe. Discounted car rentals were also perks. They could take off for a long weekend and fly from New York to Paris and be back on the job on time. And they flew for the price of the tax alone.

Every business has its perks. I consulted to the largest manufacturer of carpet pads. You know, these are the felt or jute surfaces that new carpeting sits on. Pads are costly, but employees got a big discount. Not as fun as cheap vacations, but this was an advantage, an employee benefit.

Another client is in the resort-condominiums business. They facilitate vacation trades among members. Someone in Aspen wants to visit Hawaii in the winter. No problem, because there are Hawaii condo owners that want to ski. Employees of that company get to enjoy a certain number of free days in extremely fun places around the globe, for free.

When I teach "Best Practices in Negotiation," and as I've said in my book on the subject, we should always be on the lookout for *money equivalent*s. These are perks that can be traded or received in lieu of cash.

When my dad worked with famous DJ Wolfman Jack, we were given a triple black Mustang convertible to drive. It was a trade for radio time, and no cash changed hands. But it certainly was currency of sorts, a money equivalent, and it made being in the radio sales business a lot sweeter.

If you work for Disney, you'll get discounts at their theme parks and on a lot of merchandise. Teach at many universities, and you and your family will get reduced tuition.

Which raises this question: why would any of us want to work at a place with *zero* perks?

Your company manufactures and sells household brushes. How many discounted or free brushes can you use? All other things being equal, you're going to feel better and live better by hooking up with a company that has something nice to offer you as an employee.

Consider this as you send out your résumé for the next sales post. What would you really like to sell? What would you enjoy tremendously? Maybe it's jet leasing, and you'll be able to hitch rides for free!

The right perks can fatten your wallet by making your earnings go farther, and in style. When I was growing up, my dad took me to Angels games, nearly as many as we wanted to attend. We sat next to the broadcasting booth, a great perch, for free. We earned that perk because my father worked for the same company that broadcast the games.

Tip 51: Why Not Strike Out on Your Own?

One of the recurring implicit themes we've encountered is that as a salesperson, you simply cannot trust your employers. What seems perfectly rational to them seems perfectly irrational to you.

While you may believe you're on the same team, you're not. They're on Team Profit, and you're on Team Loss. They see you as an expense, and you know what management does with expenses? They cut them.

Your territory will get cut. Your commission rate will be cut. Sooner or later, just because they can, they'll cut you. They'll hire a consultant who will convince them to take a solidly middle- to upper-middle-class job opportunity and shrink it into a McJob. These moves are almost inevitable, except in the most uniquely enlightened firms.

Google can and will pay exceptionally well because it is talent-hungry. It wants to hire and retain the best and the brightest. And in the world of Internet search, Google has no significant competitors, at least at this writing. But that can change.

In most other companies, which sell widgets in a world where widgets are available everywhere, competition means there will be downward pressures on wages.

When widgets were new to the scene, and you could only buy them from the Monolith Widget Company, there may have been a good living to be made selling for that firm. But like days described in the old song— "Summertime and the livin' is easy, fish are jumpin', and the cotton is high"—those days are no longer.

Unless, that is, you're the fifth person hired at a start-up that is bound to change the world, and they gave you stock options.

This brings me to my point. As a salesperson, you'll be taking on business risks, especially if you're paid on a straight commission basis. If you sell, you'll eat.

Why not take on ALL of the business risks and earn all of the profits?

Great sellers always face this question at some point in their careers. They tire of the politics. They tire of the treatment. They tire of the job turnover. Then they turn to themselves.

My first glimpse of the possibilities came when I sold ballpoint pens by the gross on a commission basis.

I "bought" the pens from the company at 16 cents and marked them up to 33 cents, pocketing 17 cents. I chose whom to sell to and when to sell them. Our "lists" were not sophisticated or expensive. In fact, they were free. We used Yellow Pages directories, which were lodged in large shelves against the wall. I selected my own categories to contact.

That job showed me that selling is 90 percent of a company's success. You can have great products and wonderful people, but if no one can successfully move that product, you're doomed.

Likewise, if you are simply a "me too" company, with no unique claim to fame or competitive advantage, but your salespeople are effective and motivated, you can conquer the world.

At some point you're going to ask yourself, "Why am I working for these stiffs?" My professor Peter F. Drucker said an ideal company spends as little time as possible maintaining internal relations. Apple polishing and politicking are limited, and the greatest amount of effort is reserved for being outward-looking. Getting and taking care of customers are the most important tasks. In fact, Drucker said the number-one job of every company "is the creation of a customer." Isn't that what salespeople are doing—creating customers?

This makes salespeople the most important folks in every enterprise, yes?

While managers and owners downplay your importance, they realize you're doing the heavy lifting, and they resent you for it. They cost-justify their own existence by getting in your way, making it difficult for you to be completely outward-focused. They don't want superstar sellers. They want a crew of slightly better than average sellers that have no clout. They're hammers looking for nails.

At some point, you may very well conclude that you don't want to be a nail anymore.

When I was in my fifth year of college teaching, already with substantial sales and sales-management experience under my belt, I decided to change how I taught and for whom, and at what rate of pay.

I realized I had no hope of growing rich as a traditional professor. Yes, if I published the leading texts in the field, or if I moonlighted for huge bucks as a consultant, I could improve my lot. But this would come with a heavy price tag: exhaustion.

I decided to sell my teaching by the day and not by the semester. I would sell to colleges of continuing education. They served adults, who could hire me to consult. Instead of working at one school, I'd work for dozens simultaneously.

That first call that I made, to the first university, was the hardest. They said OK, they'd run my seminar. After that, it grew a lot easier.

I did the math. I was going to earn a lot more than my traditional professor's salary. And I was going to have a lot of freedom and free time to boot.

As I mentioned before, I ended up earning ten times my teaching salary within the first eighteen months of being on my own. While I had to please dozens of partners, at least in theory, it was a lot easier than pleasing a tenure committee for seven years. And if I lost one sponsor, I could always pick up another to take its place.

You may follow this lead because you have to. Your company may "retire" you against your will. Or you'll add up all of your downtime from job seeking, and you'll conclude that you may as well stay busy selling for yourself.

One of the happiest neighbors I had was a manufacturer's representative. He sold for several companies at the same time, companies that didn't have their own dedicated sales teams. He did well enough to take several trips each year to Europe and to the Orient.

That is one way to become independent. There are others.

By chance or by choice, you may want to strike out on your own.

It may be the best way to fatten your wallet.

Tip 52: Closing Is Great, but Make Sure to Open Them First

Read the ads for salespeople, and you're bound to find these words: "Closers wanted!"

Closers, of course, are people that are ready, willing, and able to ask for the order. More importantly, they DO ask for it, and often more than once.

Closing is three things: a skill, a habit, and a reflex. You need to know how to close and which closes to use. I have detailed some closes for you, such as the assumptive-checkback close, also known as a *tie-down*: "So let's get under way, and I'm sure you'll be pleased, OK?"

The power-assumptive close follows the same pattern, but the "OK?" is removed: "So let's get under way, and I'm sure you'll be pleased."

The choice close is a perennial favorite, because it gets people to choose one version or another. Choosing nothing is not an option: "So let's get under way. The calendar indicates Monday will work, or will Tuesday be better?"

I ran across a book that delineated over a hundred closes that work. Closing requires the skill to select and use the best ones for each situation.

Closing is also a habit. You do it because you do it, and it works. It becomes part of your routine, like saying hello or asking a person how the day is going for them.

A close needs to be scripted, built in to what you do. The adage "Remember your ABCs: Always Be Closing" applies.

Closing is also a reflex. When you hear an objection, and you have reached a point in the exchange where the person has enough information to buy, then you reflexively close.

"I feel this is too much to pay!" says the prospect.

"Well, I appreciate that, and most folks feel that way initially. But they find it saves them a ton in the long run, *so let's get under way, and I'm sure you'll be pleased, OK?*"

Answering an objection without closing is a waste of time. Appending one to another becomes a reflex.

Nevertheless, we can invest so much energy in closing people that we forget to properly open them up. People need to feel a powerful urge or need or desire to purchase. If they do not, then all of the closing effort expended will not help you to ring up a sale.

How are they thinking of using your product? What are they using now? What do they like about it? What would they improve?

I drove a diesel station wagon for a number of years and it served me well. When I went shopping for a different car, the seller asked me what I had been driving, and I told him.

"Why are you looking at convertibles?" he asked with a smile.

"I've had it with being practical. I need something a little more exciting and a whole lot faster!"

"Well, this is it, isn't it?" he asked, and I just nodded.

Need meets close—that's what happened. He got me to open up, to express my desire and the need to make a change. And then he closed off of it, and there was no going back.

Don't get me wrong: closing is great. But the justification to close will be provided by the prospect. You'll elicit that by opening them up first.

Tip 53: Provide Yourself with a Proper Work-and-Life Balance

It has been said that selling is the easiest job if your work it hard, and it can be the hardest job if you work it easy.

That may be true. I can say that selling can be a great lifestyle job. Previously I urged you to hook up with employers that provide you with perks. Car allowances, free or subsidized airfare and hotels—I've mentioned more than a few advantages you can seek.

But a decent sales job will also provide you with *flexibility*. This is the essential ingredient in creating a proper work-and-life balance.

Say you need to drive your kid to see the doctor. This can produce a crisis for someone who needs to account for every second of her working day, but most salespeople can justify these sojourns because their jobs are measured differently. They're not based only on time of butt in chair.

If you measure up and you're selling, you're valuable. A company is going to cut you some slack. Deep down, though they pretend otherwise, they know you are a different breed if you're in sales. You cannot or simply will not completely throw your lifestyle out the window to sell their widgets. You can sell widgets anywhere. If they push too hard, or fence you in too tightly, you'll bolt.

You need to set limits, because most of the companies I've known will push you beyond yours. You'll offer an inch, and they'll try to grab the proverbial mile.

This means turning off your cell phone and making yourself unavailable for messaging. This also entails mixing up your working hours.

A lot of work can be done in your pajamas. Do whatever it is when you're comfortable.

Flexibility equals compensation. It may not pay you in dollars and cents, but lifestyle perks provide psychic income. They're stress reducers.

I smile when I hear the phrase *work-and-life balance*, because it suggests that working and life are two different things.

Working IS living. We cannot be machines at work and humans at home.

Sales work gives us a chance to achieve lots of satisfactions. We meet new and interesting people. They persuade us, and we persuade them. If things go well, we all prosper and are richer for our interactions. If we're not enjoying the job (and I don't mean every aspect of it), we are definitely misplaced or doing things wrong.

You have to be able to turn the job off, or at least to dial it down to a whisper. If you cannot, sooner or later you and that job will part company.

Tip 54: Don't Let Them Turn You into a Clerk!

There used to be a person in nearly every business who was the first to be hired. It wasn't a salesperson. This person answered phones, received clients and guests at the door. She or he typed correspondence, created and maintained the information system, and was the administrative glue that held the enterprise together.

This person was called a secretary.

Like *Wild Kingdom* chronicling the disappearance of a species, it is hard to find secretaries anymore. They were made extinct largely because of office automation. When everyone was given a computer, everyone was also given a keyboard. Soon everyone was expected to type his own letters, store and retrieve information, and stay organized.

Along came enterprise software. Now all were expected to share and continuously update information in real time.

Slowly but surely, we all came to be tethered to these systems. Today you simply cannot be a salesperson without using Salesforce or some other program for keeping track of clients and prospects.

This has come at a greater cost to sales productivity. Sellers spend more and more time servicing the machine—and by that I mean by entering and updating data and files—than we do servicing the clients that the files describe.

The ratio of sales to clerical time has been shrinking steadily. If you aren't careful, that sales job you were

ostensibly hired to do will morph into a 99 percent clerical routine. You'll become—that's right—a secretary.

Extinction of your sales skills is one thing that
will occur. Selling is a use-it-or-lose-it occupation.
We get sharp and stay sharp through practice, and I
don't mean typing practice. I mean closing practice—
getting people to make affirmative and profitable buying decisions.

Most CRM software enslaves us to archiving information for others in our organization to retrieve. Some
of this is necessary and even helpful. But if your communications face inward instead of outward, you aren't
selling. Maybe you're informing, explaining, and justify-
ing, but your colleagues cannot buy from you. Only real
prospects and customers can do it.

If 90 percent of your attention is facing the wrong
way, how can you or your firm prosper?

We're complicit in this conspiracy to turns sales into
clerical work. We tell ourselves we need to document
everything, that it is supremely important.

Horse feathers! More often than not, it is gilding the
lily.

Parkinson's Law states that the time to do a task, any
task, will increase to meet the time allotted for its com-
pletion. This means if you keep allocating endless time
for documentation, there will be no end to documentation!

And exactly no time will be left for selling.

Tip 55: Want Better and More Profitable Clients? Do This

In a perfect world, we'd invest our time only with those that are ready, willing, and able to buy. Time wasters would be ignored or, even better, we'd foist them upon the competition to darken their doorsteps.

We can't know who will or won't buy in advance, but we can provide incentives to those that can make speedy decisions.

Certainly our firms can offer cash incentives. Buy now and save 10 percent!

But we can also tell clients several things that will prompt them to be, well, more prompt.

We can put "Offer good until" dates on the contracts we send out. This suggests urgency and scarcity. It appeals to those that fear losing. We can also say that there is a pending cost increase, if there really is one. And we can explain, "We keep our costs down because our customers make prompt decisions. The longer it takes to come aboard, the more it costs for everyone, because those inefficiencies are passed on, right?"

This says, "Sit or get off the chair. Don't dally."

The airline industry is famous for extending discounts to those that buy well in advance of their flight dates. You can do it too. Or you can make it uncomfortable for those that want to dicker with you or to sit on the fence.

It is a fact that every follow-up you make costs you some time and effort, and our reserves of time and energy are limited. The person that costs twice as much to close is by definition half as profitable, correct?

Bad customers—the 20 percent that command 80 percent of your time—need to be identified, and you need countermeasures to handle them. (I can think of three right now. They're too needy. They insist on getting updates on top of the updates.) At the end of day, they're just not worth the time they suck from you.

Tell them you're going to be less accessible, or that you'll have to put a surcharge on their accounts for extra attention and maintenance. Call it a service surcharge. They can void it by being less needy, or they can pay.

If these options don't work, these customers can be ignored. With any luck, they'll burden someone else!

Tip 56: In a Slump? Blame the Bat!

Imagine you are in one of those endless droughts. You haven't written a good deal in a long while, and it's getting to you. You don't want to do anything with family or friends. You're no fun. Food doesn't taste right. Your energy is sapped. You feel every ache and pain. And that parched throat signals a cold is coming on.

It is a perfect prescription for self-pity and self-blaming. But this is the opposite of what you need to do to get out of a slump.

The legendary New York Yankee Yogi Berra, who had a Zen take on nearly every question, was once asked about slumping.

"Yogi, do you blame yourself when you're in a slump?"

"No way," Yogi said. "I blame the bat!"

I've always loved that line. Blaming the bat is a very constructive thing to do, according to many psychologists. You don't want to get down on yourself, because that can push you deeper down the rabbit hole of despair.

If you blame the bat, you can throw that one away and select another. But you can't throw *you* away. You are going to need to be your own best pal to get back into the groove.

We're told to take responsibility for our actions. So every sinew of your adult being could dislike bat blaming. It seems like a cheap excuse. Bats don't swing themselves; people swing them. Professionals are held to the highest performance standards because they're paid a ton to make the difficult appear easy and routine. Same for sellers, correct?

You can't control lots of things. For instance, your prospects might be thrust upon you.

And they might hit you with a bunch of objections.

But like a hitter, you can decide what sort of swing you're going to put on a ball. You can choose which pitches to whiff at and which ones to leave alone.

Why alibi when things aren't going your way? You take credit for the times things go the other way, when you're on a winning streak, don't you?

Is it fair and mature to blame the bat? Maybe it isn't, but as Yogi explained, "Who am I going to blame: ME?"

Downing yourself is fruitless if you need to feel good about your product. When we seem downcast, who wants to do business with us?

Other losers may help us, but there aren't that many of them in the ranks of professional buyers to earn us a living. If you come across all wimpy and hangdog, prospects are going to think you don't believe in your product. If you have doubts, they will mirror them.

The best attitude is that circumstances have temporarily conspired to prevent you from closing deals. But like the weather, circumstances always change, often for the better.

Stay positive until that happens, and happen it will.

If necessary, pick another bat!

Tip 57: Distinguish the Cherries from the Pits

I have only attended one seminar on how to become a business consultant, but it was a good one. It featured a speaker whose clientele included stockbrokers and wholesalers of mutual funds.

With seminars like this, you hope to glean at least one gem from the proceedings. I think I beat that. I got two or three from that meeting. The one I want to share with you pertains to cherries and pits and being able to distinguish between the two.

Cherries are juicy, nutritious, and life-sustaining. In selling, cherries are your grade-A prospects. They're high-potential and high-yield. Your time invested with them can help you to pay the bills. Indeed, they're lucrative enough to enable you to afford a frill here and there, like a nice vacation.

In this scheme, there is only one other kind of prospect in this scheme—the pits. They are none of the things that cherries are. They aren't high-yield, they're no-yield or extremely low-yield. They cannot sustain you. In fact, if you pursue them too long, they'll steal your job from you. You won't make your quota.

They don't pay bills. In a sense, they worsen them by taking your eye off of their opposites, the cherries.

Pits may have been cherries once. You'll find a large number of them in the inactive-account file. They paid someone's bills long ago, but that was long ago.

Because there are lots of inactive accounts available, if your business has been in business for a while, you'll easily be able to clog your pipeline with pits. You don't want to do this, because there will be no room for cherries.

Pit polishing is the worst thing you can do. This is taking inordinate amounts of time to buff up these inedible orbs and bring them to a gorgeous shine. No matter how shiny you make them, they will never become cherries again.

I have to share this for the simple reason that pits are nice to speak to. They have no profits to offer, but they pay their way into our calendars by being affable.

The cherries-and-pits concept is to systematically go through your prospecting base. Unflinchingly toss out the pits!

You know who some of them are. You just don't want to admit it.

Admitting they're pits brings about the epiphany that you've wasted every single second with them. So what!

Do it now. You'll be feasting again in no time!

Tip 58: You Can Get Rich Working for Someone Else, If . . .

I grew up hearing that statement: you'll never get rich working for someone else. I think it's generally true. Most businesspeople don't try to make their employees rich. It isn't their chief concern. Yet if you think about it, maybe they should. We're all creatures of incentives. Behavior results from consequences. If you want me to make you rich, help me to become rich.

But this philosophy isn't widespread. Pay a pittance and get a lot seems to be the goal.

Even so, you can grow rich working for other people. Take Tim Cook, presently the CEO of Apple and successor to founder Steve Jobs. Cook's dad was a shipyard worker. His mom worked in a pharmacy. Cook went to Auburn University and got into the computer business. When Apple was slumping, he came aboard, taking a risk, because he was working for the then more secure Compaq. Working his way up the ladder, acquiring stock options along the way, Cook is on track to become a billionaire. That's rich in my book, and he did it working for someone else. Lots of corporate CEOs have similar biographies. So it's possible.

The second way to get rich is by learning on the job, by keeping your eyes and ears open. Every business has its secrets, its special insights into marketing and product delivery. You can take these trade skills and open your own shop. Then you aren't working for someone else. You've graduated. Now it is time to cash in on what you know.

The third way is to live on a small amount of your sales earnings and invest the rest. Buy real estate. Invest in equities. Garner those things that aren't going to deflect you from pursuing your main squeeze, which is selling.

Dr. Srully Blotnick studied the career paths of people over a twenty-plus-year period. He reported his findings in a book titled *Getting Rich Your Own Way*.

Most people think they need to hitch up with a hot industry or company, like Apple. But according to Blotnick, there are numerous occupational paths to riches. He found that almost all wealth earners stuck with an occupation or a field that they loved. They ended up becoming really, really good at whatever it was. Before too long, the world detected their expertise and uniqueness, and they were then paid a premium for their work and their products.

If you examine various fields, you will see that there are at least a few very top people in them that are compensated very richly indeed. Preachers are usually people of humble means, having chosen to serve a higher purpose, but there are famous church folks that earn incredible livings.

The same can be said for teachers, as I've discussed. When I was teaching college by the semester, I struggled. Then I turned to career education, vending my lectures by the day, and I was paid ten times as much almost immediately. There are Nobel Prize winners that earn big money at universities where mere lecturers barely get by.

Blotnick noticed that formal education wasn't the distinction that separated rich from average. Those with high-school diplomas or college degrees fared equally over the long run. The key was sticking to something you love and getting really good at doing it.

If you love selling, that's great. Stick to it. There's nothing wrong with looking for oil right under your feet. Dig deeper than others, and keep that grin on your face. You could end up with a gusher.

Tip 59: Chop Wood and Carry Water. Repeat

Selling is so easy that it's hard.

Perhaps it would be more fitting to say it's simple instead of easy. Selling is so simple that we feel an urge to complicate it. Repeatedly giving in to that urge, we repeatedly shoot ourselves in the wallet.

When I say selling is simple, this is to say there are basic and limited steps involved in the process. Selling includes the four-part anatomy of a sale, which is the skeleton of a sales talk. You have the *opener*, the *description*, the *close*, and the *confirmation*.

In the broader sales process, we start with *suspects*. They are people that could buy, and typically they've been assembled in list form. The next step is to ferret out the prospects, people that are more likely to buy than the mere *suspects*. This is going to happen through some sort of contact and qualification process. We might advertise to get them to write in, click on an Internet ad, or call us. By doing that, they express interest, and suddenly we know pretty much whom to contact first. We prioritize those that have expressed an immediate need or a strong interest. Now that they're genuine prospects, we need to turn them into buyers.

This is where the anatomy of a sale comes in handy.

We pitch them, plain and simple.

Some buy right away, not many, perhaps, but some. Others need to be nudged again and again until they move into the sold column.

The remaining prospects fail to make it through the process. They're the unqualified, the rejects, people that buy from our competitors instead, and the hopelessly distracted.

To an extent, I've melded marketing with selling to make the model easier to understand. You can distinguish the two in this way. The function of marketing is to target who our prospects are out of the vaster universe of suspects. Marketing gets those people to call us, or it provides us with a rifle-shot method for reaching out to them.

Salespeople deliver the specific value proposition that our company is offering to a given prospect, customizing the message to have maximal appeal.

While there is a role for creativity in selling, this is really more the province of marketing. Selling is very Zenlike. Zen folks say a good way to reach enlightenment, which is deep understanding, is to simply chop wood and carry water. In other words, great insights come through doing the mundane, the common. Do the everyday tasks that are in front of you. Find your Zen there, they say.

The same precept applies quite nicely to selling well, with a sense of great satisfaction. Do the simple process, keeping it very basic.

Someone said there is genius in simplifying. We need to make things as simple as they can be, but no simpler. Don't leave out any parts. Don't skip around. Keep the sequence the same.

The results will take care of themselves.

Tip 60: Work the Law of Large Numbers

Imagine walking into a casino with unlimited chips at your disposal. What game would you play to have a sure winner?

It wouldn't be blackjack, because there are several ways to lose, no matter how much you bet on a single hand. The dealer can get twenty-one or can simply get a higher score than yours. You could ask the dealer to give you too many cards, which puts you out by making your hand come to more than twenty-one.

There's certainly one game where you would be assured of winning, and that's roulette. If you cover all of the numbers with chips, you'll win. I'm not saying this is an ideal way to bet. But if you bet enough, something has to pay off.

I'm an advocate of putting the law of large numbers to work in selling and in most careers. In fact, I believe in it so much that I have a best-selling audio program published on the subject: "The Law of Large Numbers: How to Make Success Inevitable."

The thesis is simple: success becomes inevitable if you do enough of anything. Earlier I mentioned Srully Blotnick's study of those that got rich. They kept doing something so often that they succeeded over the long haul.

Do enough of anything, and you'll succeed. Do more, and you'll grow rich. Outdo even that level of activity, and you'll become a legend.

This is the open secret to the law of large numbers. Expressed in sales circumstances, this could mean, "See the people, see the people, and see the people."

I've heard that said in real estate: "Make calls and get calls. Make more calls and get more calls," and you'll succeed.

ABC: Always be closing! Repeatedly ask for the sale.

Close, close, and close some more.

Our tendency, especially when we haven't been earning much business, is to do the opposite. We cut back. While some pruning of our presentations could be helpful, certainly if they have become too long, we shouldn't cut back on the number of presentations we make.

Make more, and sell more.

I've worked with many top sellers that actually relish rejections. Their theory is the more they're rejected, the closer they are to earning the next sale.

Rejection simply cannot tolerate persistence. It gives way. It caves in. It cries, "Uncle!"

Especially if you've run into a rough patch, keep running! Don't waste time contemplating your navel. Get busy, and get busier. Working the law of large numbers is a proven way to make sales happen.

Tip 61: There Is Always a Better Sales Job Waiting for You

I've never heard a sales manager begin a meeting with these words: *"Do you realize you are the BEST salespeople in the world? No one, anywhere, can top what you do!"*

One reason I haven't heard it is simple: managers and owners don't want you to realize how good your skills are. If they let you in on this big secret, you will quickly surmise that there are greener pastures, and soon after that, you'll be grazing in them.

I'll let you in on another secret: you can only get so good at selling. There isn't all that much to master. And if you've been following my drift so far, you've noted that a critical key to success is not defeating yourself.

I have met and trained thousands of sellers, and I can tell you there is a very small gap between the best and the rest. Some have better habits. Others learned a nifty trick here or there. But salespeople are salespeople.

Let me give you a recent example. I established a sales training program at a financial-services company. At first they hired people that wouldn't follow my plan.

They went way off the script, and they never really got back on it.

So I got on the phones myself. I did my thing, word for word and inflection for inflection. And it worked beautifully.

Then more sales reps were hired. They heard me pitch, saw my results, and imitated me.

They thrived.

Once I had unlocked the secrets to success, embedded them into a simple script, and then proved that the method worked, sales took off.

Though I've seen it time and again, this environment was different because I rolled up my sleeves and became the role model. I was amazed at the speed with which rookies, people who had never made big bucks before, were raking in the cash. Suddenly they were buying motorcycles and other trinkets. They never had it so good!

They didn't need years of practice, eons of experience, or silver tongues to succeed. All they needed was a good opportunity and the means to seize it.

My grandfather wanted to prove a point to a stuffy politician. He boasted, "I can take a bum off the streets, run him for judge, and he'll win!"

I feel the same way about salespeople. I can take a minimum-wage fast-food employee who has just the slightest gift of gab, and I can make him a sales success.

It takes work, but more importantly, it takes a method. If you have a good method, you're valuable. Indeed, you're probably worth more than what you're being paid where you are.

Look around! Ply your trade elsewhere. Believe me, there is always a better opportunity for you out there!

Tip 62: In a Rut? Change Your Personal Routine

Even the most seasoned travelers complain about jet lag. But for me it can be a tonic. In fact, going to a radically different time zone can work wonders. It's not so much that I'm going to see new sights, taste different food, or mingle with exotic folks, although those things are fine and can be welcomed in their own right. It's that a change in my temporal routine alters my entire outlook for the better. Like an electric shock, it changes the functioning of my body and my mind. Expectations are shaken up. And to adapt to a different time zone or routine forces the body to stretch, to release adrenalin and probably scores of other coping chemicals. Above all, the same-old is no longer. You're suddenly in a whole different space.

Recently I went to Rome, which is nine hours ahead of my time zone. Straying in that region for a week, I played by day and worked by night. When I returned to Pacific Standard Time, I caught a few extra winks over the course of a free day. Then I went back to my prior routine without a hitch.

As a matter of fact, I was exuberant, filled with energy, and a force of nature. Surprisingly, I didn't hit a biological wall after that.

You don't have to fly twelve hours to produce this rut-busting effect. Simply change your pattern where you are. Go to sleep earlier. Or wake up three hours earlier.

Then stay awake until you have cycled through your day. You can then revert to the old clock, or stay on the new.

Any change in routine can help you to dislodge from a rut. Eat differently. Order takeout. Pick up a cookbook and follow a recipe. Take a different route to work, and not necessarily a shorter one. I have this theory that there are beautiful and ugly miles. The straightest path is usually the ugliest. Side roads are more interesting.

Change your leisure habits. Watch Scandinavian crime dramas on TV.

In my experience, a change of scene or a change of time can do the trick nicely.

You're going for some behavior that gives you a different experience. It will take your attention off of your woes and shift it to your wins.

Tip 63: Better a Day Early

I was in the car-leasing business. A prospect was asking about a Cadillac, and I certainly wanted to find one for him. Which I did, and then I pitched him on the terms, offering pretty much our standard deal.

He said, "Call me on Friday."

Dutifully I waited to the appointed day. Around ten, I phoned him.

"You're too late!" he bellowed with an oddly ironic laugh. "I bought *two* Cadillacs yesterday!"

At that early stage in my career, I didn't bring too much Zen calmness to the job. So I squelched an expletive or two, and my day was shot.

"Two cars, he bought two!" I recall chastising myself, and those words, "You're too late!" kept echoing in my head.

On that day I made a momentous decision: I'll never be late again! Henceforth, if someone said to call him Friday, I'd call on Thursday.

Every now and then, people would remark, "You're too early; I said Friday!" But I found something to be true. By Thursday, the nonbuyers had made up their minds. You could hear it in their voices, or you could ferret out their intention to not do a deal. Those that had a genuine interest would green-light the deal on Thursday, assure me it was probably a go on Friday, or give me a significant update.

Being early in my callbacks shrunk the timeline for decisions, and this is a good thing indeed. This ushered in more closed deals in less time. My productivity improved. Plus, I felt I was more in charge of the selling cycle.

It is a typical stall that nonbuyers will throw at you: "Call me next month!" You put that into your notes and calendar a call. By the time a month has elapsed, they'll have to be reminded you spoke before. They had asked for a callback to gently jettison you into oblivion.

Calling two weeks later is a better idea. If there's life in the prospect, you'll find out.

If not, you'll clear your system sooner.

I learned my lesson: it is far better to be early than late.

Tip 64: It's Too Easy to Get Spoiled

The best thing that can happen to a rookie salesperson or a veteran new to a job is to pitch the first prospect and to have that prospect say yes. This shows there is money to be made. It brightens the day. The training program you just completed and your prior experience have been vindicated. It's like a recipe: if you do and say these things, you'll get sales. The universe seems to be in complete order. You're going to pay your bills. You have found a home!

And the worst thing that can happen to a rookie salesperson or a veteran new to a job is to pitch the first prospect and to have that prospect say yes.

How can that be?

It spoils you. It sends a signal that selling whatever it is can be supereasy. In a word, you could have experienced beginner's luck. That sale could have been a fluke, a one-in-hundreds result. You won the lottery. Just don't tell yourself it was skill that rang the cash register.

The same can be said for closing a huge deal, one that provides you with an outsized paycheck. Something very powerful is reset in our heads when we experience a windfall. We adjust superfast to what we suddenly believe is a new reality. "Hey, this is the way it was meant to be!" we tell ourselves. "Now we're talking!"

If there is higher potential in your sales situation than you had previously thought, then the reset button should be pushed. Raising your expectations, at least somewhat, could be justified. But it is also possible that you'll turn into a one-hit wonder. You strode into the casino that day, put a buck into Big Bertha, and she paid off for you. Bells, whistles, and sirens signaled the arrival of you, the conqueror. You can get instantly hooked on gaming. You're a natural, and the gods love you. You could be chasing that easy payoff for the rest of your days.

In selling, it's too easy to get spoiled. You're making good money for a while, and you ratchet up your lifestyle. Gone are the old cars, old houses, and old spouses. Everything's new again. Until it isn't.

Beware of a deluge of good fortune. Better yet, take it in stride. But do not take it for granted. It can shoot a big hole into your wallet!

Tip 65: Would It Be Fair If I Made Ten Million and You Made One?

I spelled out this scenario for someone the other day, just to make a point.

"Imagine I came to you with a deal," I said. "You will earn $1 million. I'll earn $10 million. Would that be fair?"

"No!" he replied emphatically.

"But you're going to earn $1 million!" I emphasized.

"Yes, but you're getting TEN," he bristled.

"So, no deal?" I asked.

"No deal!"

"Let me get this straight. I come to you with an offer of one million bucks, but you're going to turn it down because I'll earn more?"

"That's right," he said conclusively.

A lot of people are like this. They blow up what could be a very lucrative proposition because they're upset that you're going to achieve relatively more benefits than they are.

This is a huge trap. It is called *counting other people's money*. Not only is it a distraction to worry about what others are getting, it can make you say no when you should say yes.

Let's bring this into a sales perspective. You're pitching a prospect who wants you to give him a discount. It isn't as if you haven't heard this request before. But on this particular day, for this prospect, you don't feel like giving an inch. Maybe he didn't ask you nicely enough. Or he seems to be making an ultimatum: discount this deal, or no deal!

Suddenly, preventing him from reaching his goal is a more intoxicating idea than meeting your own goal, which is to close deals, to earn *some* commissions.

It happens all the time. Believe me: I have succumbed to the desire to thwart people, even if I am shrinking my own paycheck by doing so. I try to rein in this impulse, because it is self-destructive.

Some of the greatest philosophers and theologians warn us about the perils of envy. In Buddhism, it is considered a huge distraction that needs to be overcome. The antidote, some say, is to find joy in other people's joy.

For example, let's say there are other reps that earn more than you do during a given pay period. Their names appear with the words *President's Club* next to them. They're revered for their accomplishments.

Instead of wasting your time counting their earnings, see the positive message in their success. It can be done! Bigger money can be made here. Soon it will be my turn. Ask them their secrets. Instead of bringing them down, ask them to bring you up.

With prospects, don't let deals get personal. It's only business, and in business we don't get everything we want. We have to compromise, and sometimes this involves discounting.

Don't count what they're saving. Count what you're still earning, and move on to the next deal.

In martial-arts literature, there is a saying: "If you are going to bow to someone, bow low."

Acknowledge them. Leave their success alone.

Focus on yours.

Tip 66: Use Propinquity to Build Trust and Credibility

People do business with those they trust and find credible. It pays to exploit this principle by practicing behaviors that build these positive states of mind.

One factor you can control is to escalate the number of contacts you have with prospects. The more they see your name and read about you, directly and from other sources, the more they'll feel comfortable with you. You'll become a trusted and credible source, and this will break down barriers to deal making.

I did a direct-mail campaign that was based on this principle. Instead of mailing an invitation to my seminars to only one target in a given company, such as the vice president of sales, I mailed to five or six people simultaneously.

After an organization retained me to do an onsite series of programs, my contact person said: "Something incredible happened that made me aware of your programs. On the very day that I received a mailer, four other people in my firm put the same mailer on my desk!" It was as if she kept bumping into me.

You know how that happens in life. You see someone in one place, and then unexpectedly you see them somewhere else. Before long, you come to believe that your chance meetings were somehow meant to be. A greater force is bringing you together.

My client felt that way. She didn't attribute all of those flyers to my marketing concept, and that's as it should be. Usually, when people buy, they forget how they were sold. The technique used on them escapes conscious review. Look at it as a sort of helpful amnesia.

When you can make several contacts in a short time, you'll benefit from the power of propinquity. So the idea is to schedule a number of contacts. Use various media. Email your prospects. Follow with phone calls. Send reprints of articles by conventional mail.

By the way, these days snail mail is especially attention-getting, because it is used so infrequently. That's great, because your message will be read before it is tossed, unlike so many emails that automatically go to the spam folder. Use overnight mail or priority mail, which often gets even faster attention.

Repetition is the key to most successful ad campaigns, and the same concept applies to propinquity. You become a brand very quickly. People find the familiar comforting and reassuring. Make this work to your advantage.

Tip 67: Count Your Blessings as a Salesperson

I suppose that while we grew up at their sides, we never fully knew our parents. Some aspects of my dad remain mysteries. Others I've only just begun to understand. For example, why did he choose selling as his career?

He had a formal education, and he could have practiced law. He also could have worked in management or in a number of fields. But he chose sales, and he stuck with it.

Ironically, I've done pretty much the same thing. True, I became a consultant, so I've been in my own business. But I've done sales consulting primarily, along with negotiation and customer-service training. The pivotal part of my business has been client acquisition, commonly known as selling.

I am also an attorney, and as you know, I was a college professor. I continue to teach seminars at UC Berkeley and at UCLA Extension. But selling is my passion, and the theory of selling, especially how to be more productive when doing it, has been of unending fascination to me.

Why do I feel so blessed to be in this field? Did my dad pretty much feel the same way? Many have said that when you sell, you are the closest you'll ever be to being in a business of your own. Unless, of course, you do start one, which many great salespeople have done and will continue to do.

I think a sense of independence draws many to the occupation. Especially if you work in the field, commuting or traveling to meet clients, you feel you're on your own. You certainly aren't supervised and scrutinized, as you would be if you were doing inside sales or a number of other functions. If you skip or take a two-hour lunch, who is to know?

Strictly speaking, no one *should* care, because you're measured by results, by the business you get and keep. It really isn't of consequence if it takes you six or sixteen hours a day to succeed.

Independence, or at least having the feeling you're on your own, is a great perk. Not being under someone's thumb second by second is a related benefit. To a large extent, you also set your own income. Want to earn more? That's easy. Close more business. See more people. Persist.

The perception that we're writing our own checks is another blessing. How many people can impact their own earnings from day to day or week to week?

Another blessing is that salespeople are important. You can get carried away with this, but bear with me as I explain what I mean.

"Nothing happens in a company until a sale is made!" Have you ever heard that expression? It's true. Sales are needed to get assembly lines moving and to keep them moving. Sales give the accountants something to count.

There's no customer service without customers. Sellers create customers. I could go on.

Salespeople turn the wheels of business. If you can figure out how to eliminate sellers from the loop of business, you've done quite an act of alchemy, like turning water into gold.

Some companies have tried and conspicuously failed.

Remember the General Motors unit known as Saturn? That unit famously tried to introduce a no-haggling policy into the car-buying process. You don't need sellers if buyers will buy without them, correct?

But that experiment didn't last. The cheery, hand-clapping, cultish delivery of cars, untouched by salespeople's hands, failed.

Surprise! People actually like dickering at dealerships. It's one of the few culturally sanctioned places to bargain.

The Internet portended the end of salespeople for a while. That didn't happen. It's a lot harder to try on shoes that arrive in the mail, mailing back the poor fits, than it is to do that in person, with a human helping.

Sellers are needed to explain value. Why should people pay more for a Mercedes when they can get by with a Ford?

Do you remember your best teachers? They were enthusiastic. They were inspired. They loved what they did for a living. And they probably showed you that they liked you. You soared when they smiled in your direction.

Sellers are the same way. People appreciate guidance, and this is especially the case when they're buying unfamiliar or complex or expensive items.

OK, so a certain sort of business has figured out how to get along without sellers. Maybe it is one of those car-insurance companies on the Internet. Insurance is insurance, right? It's just a matter of price.

Not true. ˙

I was consulting in Tacoma, Washington. My rental car was parked on the roof of my hotel. When I was about to go back to the airport, I noticed a huge crater in the driver's side door. This wasn't an itsy-bitsy dent. It was a half-moon.

My insurance agent with State Farm has a memorable phone number, so I dialed it from my mobile. I explained the situation.

He said, "It sounds like collision coverage to me." I had a $1000 deductible on that.

"What is collision?" I asked Jim.

"Well, it's like you ran into a tree. It's a one-vehicle crash. You did it, and nobody did it to you."

I didn't like the sound of that. "Jim, what's comprehensive, and what's my deductible on that?"

"That's like vandalism. Someone spray-paints your car. You have a $500 deductible on that."

"Well, Jim, I didn't run into a tree on the rooftop of my hotel. And somebody might have been peeved at me for parking too closely and booted my door. That would be comprehensive, right?"

He agreed, and that was the category in which my claim was filed. I had rented a car with a charge card that gave me coverage for the first $500 of damage, so I wasn't out of pocket one dime for that incident. Try persuading a faceless, nameless Internet company to give you the same result.

The blessings of selling are many. Count them, each and every day.

It will give you psychic income. And it could make your day!

Tip 68: Postulate Success!

The greatest positive thinkers have all pretty much said the same things.

If you can conceive it, you can achieve it.

You get what you think about.

Forget the past. Your point of power is the present.

I happen to agree with them, but get this: even if these are generalizations that only hold true some of the time, they are still constructive beliefs.

They are more practical than limited or negative thoughts.

Big goals are more energizing than small ones.

We know this to be true. Why else would so many people postpone gratifications in order to qualify themselves for careers? They have to believe they're going to achieve a huge payoff after such sustained exertion and sacrifices, and many do.

Unfortunately, most of us misuse our imaginations. We postulate bad results instead of good ones. The seller that thinks, "This guy will never buy!" and then curtails his efforts, allowing his energy to wane, doesn't do himself any favors.

Fostering negativity contributes to negative results. When sales fail to materialize, our bad expectations seem to always come true. A cycle is created, one that seems perpetual. "I'll never get another sale!" we start to conclude starts.

Of course, that's an irrational belief. It's very difficult to get NO sales, especially if people around you are performing. Or if you have earned them in the past, why wouldn't you earn more presently?

But that belief that you will not can determine your destiny. Possibly you'll introduce negative suggestions to your prospects, or you'll give off the impression that you don't believe your product is worth the price.

There are antidotes to these problems. When you start entertaining negative expectations, dispute them. Ask yourself, what evidence do I have that I'll never get this sale? You failed to earn the last one? But that was a different prospect, wasn't it?

Imagine success instead. Put the picture in your mind of prospect after prospect smiling and saying an enthusiastic YES! It sounds goofy, but that image is a lot more constructive than the opposite, wouldn't you agree?

If you achieve anything in life, or if you expect to stand out or be outstanding in any way, you'll attract cynics and critics. Don't help them out by becoming one yourself!

I started my martial-arts training after forty. Most of my fellow trainees were a lot younger. But I persisted, and I imagined myself achieving the black belt.

Year after year passed, and I was promoted through the ranks. I invested even more time at the dojo, and my skills increased. The great majority of people that passed through the dojo dropped out. But I remained.

I was only the twentieth person to ever achieve black belt. It took eight years to accomplish. Over thirty years, 10,000 people had flowed through the dojo, yet only twenty ascended to the black-belt level.

I did it because I imagined I could. Others had more physical ability to begin with, but mine became awesome with sustained practice.

Those that think they can are those that win.

Postulate success. When you start succumbing to images to failure, replace them immediately.

I remember speaking to the founder of our dojo, who of course is a very spiritual fellow. I was experiencing a drought in my business. I asked him for advice, though the material world wasn't of much interest to him. In fact he often derided the idea of accumulating money and driving fancy cars. This put us a little at odds, but I thought he might have some sage advice.

He said, "Postulate the outcome you want, in the same way you'd postulate being victorious in battle. If you need $10,000, then imagine it flowing to you, and then let the universe do the work."

"And if I need $100,000?" I asked with a smile.

"Do the same thing, because the amount doesn't matter."

Well, I did it. I postulated receiving $100,000 within three months.

The universe sent me a few good clients, and I met that goal.

Remember what we've covered here:

If you can conceive it, you can achieve it.

You get what you think about.

Forget the past. Your point of power is the present.

Big goals are more energizing than small ones.

Those that think they can are those that win.

Tip 69: Treat Yourself to Some Goodies

All work and no play make Jack a dull salesperson. And that's a very costly place to be.

If I feel I'm stuck in a rut, that it's Groundhog Day (as in the movie), that I'm going through the same old every day, then I'm probably headed for a breakdown.

This has been my fate several times across my career. What's interesting is that my breakdowns have come when I've been flush with cash. Sales haven't been a problem. I've had large and profitable gigs, and the bills have been paid. But success can be boring, and it can lead to burnout.

Vacations are essential if you want to stay in the game and not get sidelined.

If you are a workaholic, this might be the last thing you want to hear. I was that way one year when I took my family to Hawaii. I never stopped working. I scheduled seminars at both ends of the trip, and I was interviewed over the phone by more than twenty radio stations from my hotel room. I was lucky to swim in the pool without work intruding.

Given modern technology, we can work from anywhere, and as you know, I've done it. I'm better able to handle the work-play balance than ever before. Still, we need reminders that we are making progress.

Rewards remind us that today isn't merely a repeat of yesterday.

When people mention retiring at a certain age, I laugh. I'm never going to retire if I can help it. I enjoy what I do. Plus, I have already experienced multiple miniretirements during my career.

When I put myself through law school, I didn't close my consulting firm. I accepted only those gigs that were located within an hour and a half flight from my home airport. Surprisingly, my income didn't plummet. I was able to earn my degree, pass the bar, and feel I went into retirement, at least partially.

Investing eight years in earning my black belt was also a welcome diversion from my career. It was a perk, a benefit that gave me pleasure and endowed me with a certain toughness that enhanced my effectiveness at work.

Send yourself to some gourmet-cooking classes. (They might be on my list.) Learn another language, especially while you're doing windshield time on the way to or from seeing clients.

Upgrade that car! Do those things that say you are on your way, that signify that you have paid some dues. If you're all work and no play, you could be slowed down by something not of your choosing.

Tip 70: Keep Positive Reminders Nearby

By no means am I the only guy who likes Frederick Remington's statues.

I have two of them on my rolltop desk. One is a bronco buster, who is glued to the saddle despite every effort of his steed to dump him into the cactus. The other is a sharpshooter lining up a shot while mounted on a galloping horse.

I'm sure you've seen copies of these statues. They mean a lot to me. For one thing, they say conditions will never be perfect. Those that should be helping you, ones upon whom you rely, could be dislodging you from a secure saddle. Expect change, and roll with it. Either you become one again with that bucking bronco, or you'll be pulling needles out of your hide. You'll also be walking!

The sharpshooter is unusually serene as he takes aim. Everything else is in motion, but his eye and trigger finger are steady. This one says, set a proper goal and never take your eye off of it. Pursue it wherever it takes you. Plus, you may very well miss, so be prepared to calmly take aim again. And remember, big shots are little shots that keep shooting!

I have some martial-arts mementos here and there, as well as some favorite books that I grab for a minute for some inspiration. And there are family photos, of course.

The statues remind me of how I need to work: steadily. Amidst distractions and obstacles, I need to stay in the saddle. The martial memorabilia remind me of obstacles I have overcome. They signal persistence and working through pain and discomfort. The family photos remind me of why I work and why success is important to me.

Look around your space, especially where you work. What symbols have you placed there, and what do they mean to you?

I suggest becoming somewhat of a curator. Just as there are curators at museums, you can curate your own collection. It doesn't have to be grandiose, but it should speak to you and inspire you, while reminding you about the stuff you are made of.

Don't worry about what other people may think. This is your treasure trove. Maybe there's a sports cap from the team you cheered when you were small. Or there's a compass in the drawer that you brought to every camping trip. These are the symbols of you, the symbols of success. They remind you of why you work, how you work best, and the obstacles that you've overcome.

That's strong stuff!

Tip 71: There's Gold in Those Inactive Accounts!

I've mentioned the significance of leads several times. Their importance can be overstated, but not by much.

What right-thinking salesperson doesn't want fresh leads to contact? Who would spurn people that haven't been spoiled by countless past contacts? Leads that haven't been wooed by the competition—those pristine prospects—are there any sellers that do not crave those?

There is someone, actually. That would be me. I do love fresh leads, but in some cases, stale ones are even better. I'm referring to those accounts that purchased from your firm in the not-too-distant past. They bought what you sell. It's just that nobody has communicated with them in a long time. They're sitting in the database, gathering dust like some cast-aside lampshades or old shoes that haven't seen daylight in a year or so.

I'm speaking here of inactive accounts. Every company that has been in business for a time has them. Some have hundreds or even thousands. Each day that passes, they grow more inactive and a little staler, without good reason.

There is gold in your inactive accounts! Many of them are just waiting for you to stroll across the dance floor to chat them up.

Usually we don't put a move on them. Why? In many cases, we presume that they are hostile; they stay away because they don't like us. We mistake silence and shyness for hostility.

I'll give you an example. I was consulting for a very large clothing distributor in northern California. The assignment was for me to train people to contact the company's thousands of inactive accounts.

I did that. Part of my work product was a script. It began with a hello, and it went on to say that we had done business before but for some reason we weren't doing business currently.

When asked people why, we expected to hear various versions of "You did us wrong!" But that hardly ever occurred. Most people couldn't summon a reason for having stopped their patronage. Incredibly, we discovered that they did not consider themselves to be inactive at all. That was our label for them, not theirs.

We pivoted quickly. I changed the script to say, "We're calling to thank you for all of the business you've done with us, and as a loyalty reward, we are offering this special sale."

Wow! The results were staggering. Up to half of those that were contacted were willing to buy again. That rate of success beats what most companies can achieve with supposedly better, fresher leads. Plus, when contacting past customers and clients, you incur no new lead cost.

I instructed reps to pause after saying, "We're calling to thank you for all of the business you've done with us." Invariably prospects would respond with, "You're welcome!" and "You bet!" and "My pleasure!" These are far cries from complaints, which is what we thought we'd hear from accounts we called inactive.

You may still be sold on the thought that new leads are better. Fair enough, but the next time there is a shortage of the new, don't be bashful. Stroll across that dance floor and strike up a conversation with the silent types. Many of them are to be treasured!

Tip 72: Learn the Lesson of One Red Paper Clip

I start some of my seminars with an exercise. It's a little deceptive. I pass out a few business cards. Each has a paper clip attached to it. Some are metallic, others are green, but there is always one that is red.

My business card mentions that I do sales, customer-service, and negotiation training. It also showcases my credentials, and it says I am an attorney-at-law. All true.

"What is this item worth?" I ask.

Most respond to the question as if I am asking about the business card and what it says.

That's the sleight of hand. They're focusing on the paper, when it is the clip that contains the value, as they'll see.

I modify the question. "What is the cash value of what I handed to you?"

I hear "Zero!" a lot, along with "A few cents."

"Would you believe me if I said what I handed you is worth a speaking part in a major motion picture or a paid-for, two-story house in a nice suburb?" Of course, I've piqued their interest, and I tell them about Kyle Mac-Donald, a Canadian who got both of things. He started by trading a single red paper clip for a fish-shaped pen, and he kept trading up. You can validate this by searching for "one red paper clip" at Google. You'll be steered to Kyle's story at his website and to Wikipedia, where you'll see that nice white house he bought. (It has red trim!)

The point is that value doesn't lie in objects themselves. Value is a perception. Just as there are paintings by such masters as Van Gogh that have sold for a few dollars at garage sales, there is no solid or predictable connection between price and value. Value is in the mind.

Your job as a seller is to create enough value so the price you're asking will seem utterly reasonable or an outright bargain. If you're hearing a lot of price objections, you probably have fallen short in selling value.

One of my clients rents money. He is in the financial-services business. He makes short-term loans to small businesses. His sellers hear the price objection a lot, because he is renting his money for 50–200 percent per year, if you do the math.

"That's outrageous!" some say. They're expecting to pay a lot less for a loan.

But enough people find his value proposition appealing. Enough, that is, to afford him a decent lifestyle and to give his sellers very nice commission splits.

The key distinction between those that buy and those that don't is that the former are convinced they're getting sufficient value. Sellers have asked them, "For every dollar we supply, how many dollars do you expect to earn in return—two, three, or four?" If they select any of these replies, they're saying that they are going to meet or beat the cost of the money they're renting. That's all that counts.

Some certainly believe that the deal makes no sense, that "on principle" the money costs too much. But that is an abstraction. They think they can qualify for cheaper bucks, but in many cases they cannot. Their credit history and credit scores are flawed. They are big risks, seen from the vantage point of bankers who lend at lower rates to better credit risks. It is a matter of accepting expensive money or trying to get by with no money.

There is value in even the most apparently lopsided propositions. But that value won't jump out; it has to be teased out. The seller's role is to adjust the prospect's needs and wants to fit the products and services being sold.

That happens through a give-and-take process.

Prices, by themselves, always seem high. Even if you cut your margins in advance to the lowest possible levels, there are some customers who will announce, "You're too high."

I have news for you. Prices are never too high. The perception of value is too low.

That's another lesson from one red paper clip.

Tip 73: Create Your Own Leads

Insurance people have done it for at least a half-century that I'm aware of.

Others wait in vain for something to happen, for their managers to hand them a fish.

Better to cast your line into the water. As Ovid said, keep your line cast, because you'll find a fish in the unlikeliest of ponds.

I'm speaking about the creation of leads. As sellers, we can become too passive. We wait to be given the bait that will help us to catch the fish so we can eat.

But there's almost always a snag. That wonderful lead source that you've been used to disappears. The lake runs dry.

I saw it happen not long ago. A company depended on leads that were obtained from broadcast faxes. As it turned out, junk faxes are illegal. They're banned by the Federal Trade Commission. Lo and behold, people started complaining, the company was sued, and it had to abandon this source of leads.

You can count on a few things when it comes to leads. For one, there will never be enough. Number two, your competitors will bid up the prices of the good ones, and before long, you'll be paying more and more and getting less and less.

I was saying that insurance people create their own leads, or at least they used to. They'd ask every prospect for the names of three people who might need life or car coverage. Then those three would be contacted and asked for the same list. It doesn't take a math genius to figure that if you keep doing this, you'll never run out of warm leads to contact. By *warm*, I mean you'll be able to refer to the person who referred you, and the glow from that relationship will carry over to you.

Word-of-mouth advertising is said to be the best— one person recommending you to another. Referrals work like this. If you aren't asking for them, you're lazy or dumb or both.

True, people are not going to refer you to direct competitors, but you're smarter than to ask for that.

In the same vein, you might find a kind of ecological niche to thrive in. I told you how successful I was selling ballpoint pens to restaurant owners. I discovered that niche, and it fed me well.

Examine the customer base. What types have purchased from you more than others? Which ones have been the most profitable?

Let's say it's independent insurance agents. Lists are easily compiled online. Or if you've determined there are certain characteristics you need among those agents, such as annual revenues, you can use a list broker to supply you with leads, at a price.

There's no reason to run out of leads!

Take charge of your income by creating your own.

Tip 74: Make Cold Calls!

I mentioned that I was in the car-leasing business at age twenty-one. I didn't spell out how I earned my first sales.

I made cold calls over the phone. This was unheard of at my company. The main thrust there was to add vehicles from the existing client base, to get referrals, and to close walk-ins.

I had cut my teeth in selling by making cold calls at Time-Life, and I became the top seller on the team, so I was particularly effective at it.

Unlike the majority of sellers, who only feel comfortable with incoming leads or hot prospects, I like mine cold, at least some of the time. Here are the reasons.

First, when you bring a new idea to a fresh prospect, chances are this person is yours completely: there is no competition. You inaugurated the idea in the prospect's mind of buying your product at this time. You're not being compared to anyone else, and you're not in a bidding war. That could happen later on, once the prospect decides he or she will definitely buy. They may shop around. But initially you'll be on your own, occupying the high ground. That's a good place to be.

Second, when you cold-call, you are in an active, take-charge mode. You are "at cause" and not "at effect." You'll sound more confident and proactive than if the person contacted you.

Third, you are truly doing alchemy, transforming nothing into something, water into gold.

Let's go back to the car-leasing experience. My training manager was the same person who hired me. He would pass by my cubicle and shake his head as if to say, "You poor, misguided soul, you have no future here." It shocked him when I brought in my first contract, which was for not one, but two cars!

"Where did this come from?" he asked with a mix of appreciation and concern.

"From cold calling," I replied flatly.

"You went out and got the contracts signed in person, though, didn't you?"

"No, I mailed them, and he mailed them back."

"What are you going to do about his used cars?" was the next question.

"I'm going to buy them!" I said, as if this was the most natural thing in the world.

The deal sailed through. From that moment, I was a minor legend. Every new recruit was expected to cold-call for business.

You know that I started my seminars business by cold-calling into universities. I still have that business, which started decades ago with a single call placed to a college administrator. My current affiliations with UC Berkeley and UCLA started as cold calls.

The point is: cold calling is effective and lucrative. Don't let people tell you otherwise.

Plus, when you cold-call, you toughen yourself and sharpen your instincts. When a warmer lead comes your way, you'll be all over it.

Do it regularly. It will get you back to the basics, and you'll feel incredibly self-reliant.

Tip 75: Be Open to Constructive Criticism

I mentioned how I participated in a U.S. Navy training program that helped me to make millions of dollars during my career. In that program, I learned how to change my training approach and become successful with all sorts of adult learners. My course evaluations soared, as did my income. Without the high-grade criticism I received, I would be a lot poorer in many ways.

Most of us can't stand being criticized. Instantly we get defensive, because we feel threatened. We think our most intimate selves are being degraded by negative comments.

But it's usually about our behavior, not our egos. The more we can remove our egos from resisting criticism, the better off we'll be.

The smartest professionals in every field welcome quality feedback.

My role model for this was the congressperson I helped to get elected to office. I critiqued his speeches. When I was sitting with him and his campaign manager, he soaked in everything I said. He closed his eyes to better imagine what I was describing. He thanked me wholeheartedly for my input. I have never known anyone to accept criticism with such grace.

In selling, our only real hope for improvement doesn't come from trying harder. I mentioned the perils of "efforting," or "pressing," as my dad used to call it. I think most of us work pretty hard as it is.

Our sales achievements are going to come from working *differently*. To do this, we have to be open to examining our behaviors objectively. Others need to take an occasional look at what we're doing and offer constructive pointers.

We could be like ships: We've been in the water so long that we're unaware of the barnacles that have built up on our hulls. They need to be scraped off so we can reach better speeds, wasting less energy in the process.

As with some of the sections here, I'm sure you've said to yourself, "I knew that!" Maybe you did. It's important to be reminded now and then about what we've forgotten, or forgotten to employ.

Being open to criticism is also an exercise in humility. I know a senior vice president of marketing who said something very important to the trainees during the

Navy program I mentioned: "Nice and humble does it every time!"

He was setting a tone for our training. We should be nice and humble in our teaching tone. But it is equally important to adopt that tone when we're learning and improving.

Start by making it a goal to accept criticism with greater humility. You'll let more in, and some of it will change your income, and perhaps your career, for the better.

Tip 76: Get In and Spread Out

You never know where you're going to learn a great sales tip. It pays to keep your ears perked up so you won't miss the tips as they come along. Asking other sellers what works for them can help you a great deal. (You know that I advise you to keep *your* best techniques a secret. When it's time to share, throw out an idea everybody already knows.)

I learned a few good moves at Xerox, where I trained some top-notch producers. One of them said, with regard to selling into organizations: "Get in and spread out."

Sounds a little like a military deployment, doesn't it? You enter at a certain point. You could be visiting with a senior vice president of sales. Before finishing with that person, ask her to introduce you to her counterpart in customer service. Repeat this request with that person. By doing this, you'll have lots of shots at selling into that company, not just one. Plus, you'll be tapping several potential budgets.

Politically, it doesn't hurt to know many people and to have them pulling for your project or product. And of course your original champion might have limited clout and be unable to give you the effort or result you need. If she stumbles, you can change horses.

But remember who brought you to the dance. Keep the lines of communication open with your initial sponsor.

I recall doing am extensive program at a software company. My initial sponsor, Bob, came to one of my public seminars, and he enthusiastically brought me into the company. His boss adopted the program, because it was an obvious winner. I was able to spread out and deliver training and consulting across the enterprise.

One day the boss asked me what I thought of Bob. I could tell the superior was really hoping I'd say something negative about Bob.

"You know," I said, "I'm not comfortable making that kind of assessment. It's beyond the scope of my engagement. Plus, I'm not that objective. Bob brought me in, and so did you. If anyone asked me that question about you, I'd have to give the same answer, as you can appreciate."

You might think that is misplaced loyalty, but I do believe in the idea of honoring your sponsors, unless they have cast you adrift. You will need their testimonials at some point down the road. If you spread out during your time at the firm, you may be fortunate in having a number of supporters later on.

Tip 77: Would You Rather Be Right or Rich?

Looking over my sales career, the many mistakes I have made, and the countless ways I've shot myself in the wallet, I see a pattern. This is a pattern that I've only recently started to break.

Before I detail it for you, let me mention that I have invested a lot of time becoming an expert. I define an expert as someone that knows more about a topic than most others, and he knows he knows.

If you've been selling for a while, you may be an expert in this area. You may also be an expert on your product or service. But if you come across as arrogant or superior, you're going to tee off the people that should welcome that expertise.

One thing we'll never really be an expert at is seeing value from the viewpoint of our clients. We don't know what's good for them. In this one department, they're the experts.

For example, I did a major contract at a well-known consumer electronics firm. I taught their customer service personnel how to sell add-on products to angry customers. I developed a really masterful blueprint, which necessitated a lot of original thinking. I drew upon my advanced training in communication and psychology to break new ground.

My techniques performed amazingly well. About 50 percent of those customers that were treated to my communication design bought add-on products during their original complaint call. Crucially, their satisfaction increased.

Other people in the world may have been able to achieve what I did, but at that time, you couldn't convince me of it.

My sponsor at the company wanted to introduce my techniques on a voluntary basis. This meant some customer-support reps could opt out of using the tools if they weren't completely comfortable.

To me, this was preposterous. It was a public company, and it was accountable to shareholders, and it was turning down a chance to really drive up its profits. They wanted to snatch defeat from the jaws of victory!

I requested a meeting with senior managers. I spelled out my position: that it was ill-advised to use my methods on a voluntary basis. With a sure winner, they should compel compliance.

Here's what happened. They expressed appreciation for my efforts, and they agreed with the results. But their culture at the company provided associates with this privilege to opt out. They would pay me to come back over a period of months. I could use friendly persuasion to get more compliance.

Returning would not have been a lifestyle sacrifice for me. I lived very well on the road at the time, and I had friends in the area. The city in which they were located was filled with fun diversions.

But I decided it was better to take a stand. I knew irrationality, and this was it! I was the expert. I had created an expert system, and I knew if management didn't reinforce it, the jungle would reclaim the airstrip. All traces of my great achievement would be obliterated in no time.

Looking back, I understand the position I took, but I was the one being irrational.

I preferred being right to being rich!

Today I would have made a different choice. I would have understood that to my client, value was not maximizing profits; it was maximizing comfort for its own employees. Where the profit motive conflicted with the comfort motive, comfort would win.

I saw this as corporate corruption, as misfeasance, as ineptitude. But value for me wasn't in maximizing corporate profits either. I was using my clients' sites as laboratories where I could experiment with new sales and service technologies.

There was a huge benefit in this, because I popularized some of my new methods in books and seminars. I also had a private reserve of techniques that I would license my clients to use and that I chose not to popularize.

I wanted proof that I had hit an intellectual and practical grand-slam home run, and those opt-outs were preventing me from realizing my rightful glory and rewards.

My place was not to critique the management of my program. That was their business. It was their privilege to buy a pair of shoes and never wear them, to purchase a classic car and to keep it in the garage. They paid me, and that's pretty much the only duty they had.

From the decision they made to allow profits to not accumulate, I prophesied doom for that firm. Fast-forward a few years. I was right. It went bankrupt. It failed to adapt quickly enough to the digital revolution.

Peter F. Drucker, my late professor and management sage, told a story in the classes we had together. His niece was turning eight years old, so he bought her a gift. He used this gesture as a way of explaining how value is a perception that our customers own. If we want to prosper, we need to align ourselves with their idea of value to the extent we can. When we're successful at this alignment, what we think of as selling becomes less and less significant. We don't have to push or use trickery to succeed.

Drucker presented his niece with a beautifully boxed and bowed brassiere—her first. He explained, "She had no practical purpose to which she could put it, of course. But that didn't matter. She was thrilled because it made her feel grown-up. That was 'value' to her."

Though by dint of experience and learning, I have more expertise than I've ever had, I feel less and less of a need to be right, to insist that my viewpoint prevail.

Perhaps I've finally accepted the wisdom in the saying, "The customer is always right." Whether or not we agree with the customer's view isn't the point.

Would *you* rather be right or be rich? I know what my answer is.

Epilogue

We've come to the end of our discussion. I hope you have found it useful in diagnosing some of your strengths and weaknesses in selling. I know I have.

The great author George Orwell said, "I write to clarify my own thinking." This is partly true for me too.

I'm a professional speaker, I sell everyday, and I consult and coach every day as well.

If you or your company would like to have me address your challenges in selling, negotiating, or providing top customer service, simply let me know. Feel free to contact me at (818) 970-GARY, which is (818) 970-4279, or by email at one of my several email addresses, including gary@ drgarygoodman.com and gary@customersatisfaction.com.

CPSIA information can be obtained
at www.ICGtesting.com
Printed in the USA
LVHW011923030419
612848LV00015B/154/P

9 781722 501945